690
BA

Baldwin, Ed

Building outdoor
structures

DATE		
FEB 23 1985	NO 6'90	
MAR 23 1985	MY 18'91	
MY 11 '85	MY 1'92	
JE 3 '85	APR 25 '94	
AG 6 85	JN 01 96	
DE 21 85	JL 27 96	
AP 3 86	JN 02 97	
AP 27'87	OC 15 '99	
MY 06'88	SE 10 '02	
AG 11 '88	AP 05'06	
JA 3 '89	MY 07'10	

⊕ THE BAKER & TAYLOR CO.

Building
Outdoor
Furniture

A Family Workshop Book
By Ed & Stevie Baldwin

CHILTON BOOK COMPANY
Radnor, Pennsylvania

Copyright 1984 by The Family Workshop, Inc.
Published in Radnor, Pa. by Chilton Book Company
Library of Congress Catalog Card Number: 83-45383
ISBN: 0-8019-7502-6
Manufactured in the United States of America

Created by The Family Workshop, Inc.
Managing Editor: F. Van Huntley
Editorial Director: Janet Weberling
Editors: Rob Dickerson, Mike McUsic, Rhonda Mulberry
Art Director: Dale Crain
Production Artists: Christopher Berg, Roberta Taff, Wanda Young,
                    Janice Harris Burstall, Verna Stonecipher-Fuller
Typography: Deborah Gahm, Karl Lauritzen
Creative Director: April Bail
Workshop Director: D.J. Olin
Woodworkers: Charles Henley, Mike Garrett
Photography: Bill Welch
Project designs: Ed and Stevie Baldwin, D.J. Olin, April Bail

1 2 3 4 5 6 7 8 9 0   3 2 1 0 9 8 7 6 5 4

This book is dedicated to Sue B. Puckitt, honorary member of the family, with heartfelt thanks for her friendship and encouragement.

Preface

In producing this book we designed and built many more pieces of outdoor furniture than you will find between these covers. After much discussion, appraisal of the techniques involved, and testing of the pieces themselves (one of our editors would have spent more than two hours testing the chaise lounge if we hadn't awakened him), we settled on the final projects to be included. We hope that you will find them as attractive and comfortable as we do; we know you will find them extremely easy to build.

The book begins with a section on tips and techniques for buying and working with wood and with PVC pipe. We strongly recommend that you read this section before beginning a project. For the beginner it will provide basic information on materials, tools, and terminology. For the experienced builder, who knows, we might just possibly be able to teach you a new trick!

Each project plan contains a list of required materials and provides thoroughly illustrated step-by-step instructions for building that particular item. Most projects can be built using common hand and/or hand-held power tools. In some cases, we did use shop tools (table saw, planer, etc.) to speed the process: please remember, folks, we had to produce all twenty-one pieces of furniture in a very short time.

We would like to offer special thanks to a number of individuals and companies who provided materials, services or tools for building the projects. The Danish oil which provided such a fine finish for our furniture was supplied by Watco-Dennis Corporation. The tools supplied by Shopsmith and Black & Decker performed like champions. A special note of appreciation is due Stephen Ward Smith who provided the luxurious greenery you see in the photos as well as his considerable expertise in landscaping.

Our patio and yard, as well as those of our co-workers, are now furnished with the easy-to-build furniture you will find in this book. We are looking forward to a great deal of outdoor relaxation this summer as well as a lively schedule of outdoor entertaining. We hope that you can join us, at least in spirit, by enjoying your own outdoor creations.

Contents

Tips & Techniques

Practically every woodworker with more than a few week's experience has his or her own favorite ways of performing the more common procedures involved in building things from wood. This is not an attempt to persuade you away from your own tried-and-true techniques, but rather is intended to provide some essential information concerning the materials, terms, and techniques that we used for the projects in this book. Some of the information may be old hat to you – some may be new – some you may disagree with. If there's one thing we know for certain about woodworking, it's that everyone approaches it a bit differently.

The information provided in this section is geared toward outdoor construction. The recommended adhesives and wood finishes, for instance, are not necessarily the same ones we would use for indoor furniture. Included here you'll find discussions of various types of lumber, preservatives and finishes, adhesives, fasteners, joints, and some miscellanea that will be helpful in using this book. At the end of the woodworking tips you'll find information on buying and working with PVC plastic pipe, which we used for a few of the projects. If you've never worked with PVC before, you'll be surprised at how simple it is and at how attractive the results will be. We suggest that you read the Tips & Techniques all the way through, or at least scan them, before you begin work on any project.

WOODWORKING TIPS

Selecting Wood

Different types of wood often have vastly different characteristics. This makes certain woods better for specific purposes than others. In addition, lumber is graded according to quality. We'll talk about types of wood for outdoor construction first, then we'll discuss the grading system.

Woods are divided into two general categories: hard and soft. Most hardwoods are much more difficult to cut and work with, but usually are more sturdy and long-lived than softwoods. Teak and oak are two hardwoods recommended for outdoor construction, with the latter being easier to come by as a general rule. Teak must be imported and is quite expensive. Softwoods are a lot easier to work with. The most commonly available are fir, redwood, hemlock, cedar, cypress, larch, spruce, and pine. Douglas is a particularly good fir; pine usually is available in both white (finer grain) and yellow (coarser grain).

Softwoods vary widely in their tendency to shrink, swell, and warp. Those least likely to do so are redwood, white pine, spruce, cedar, and cypress. Of these, cypress is more difficult to work with than the others and spruce is less decay resistant. Part of what makes a board more or less rot resistant is the portion of the tree from which it is cut. **Figure A** illustrates the difference between a heartwood board and one that is cut farther from the center of the tree. The more densely-packed annual rings near the center of the tree produce a highly rot resistant board, while boards cut from farther out may offer very little resistance, even when the stock is redwood or cedar. At the lumberyard, examine the ends of the boards carefully. The pattern of and distance between rings will tell you a lot about how long your outdoor furniture will last.

In the materials list for each project in this book we have specified the type of wood we used. We worked

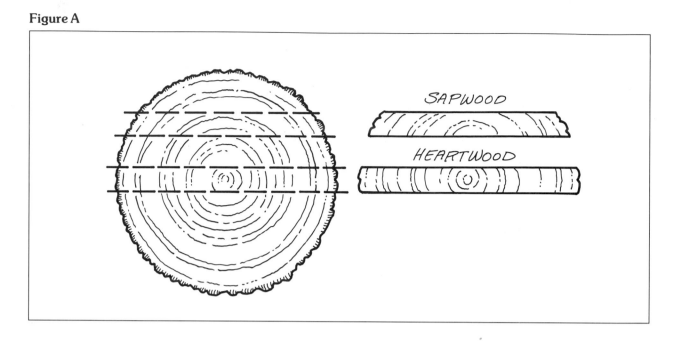

primarily with redwood, and sometimes oak. You may prefer to use other types of wood.

Lumber is graded, as we mentioned earlier. We have provided a rundown of the grading system for pine, which is also used for most other types of lumber. Keep firmly in mind that you need not use the highest grade of lumber for every (or any) project. As a matter of fact, for outdoor furniture you can get away with a much lower grade than what would be appropriate for fancy indoor furnishings. In most of our redwood projects, for example, we used #2 common construction grade lumber. If you are in doubt as to which grade to use for a specific project, talk it over with your lumber dealer. Show him the plans so he gets the whole picture.

#5 common – Full of knots, knotholes, and other headaches but the least expensive, this grade of lumber should be used only when structural strength is not required and when you intend to paint. It is prone to check (crack along the grain), and usually will not be as thoroughly seasoned or dried as the higher grades.

#4 common – This grade is low in cost and has lots of imperfections, but less so that #5. It is good for fences and other outdoor uses in which appearance is not crucial.

#3 common – Small knotholes are common and knots are sometimes easily dislodged while you work. This is a better grade than #4 or #5, but is still prone to check.

#2 common – This grade should be free of knotholes but still has its share of knots. It is often used for indoor flooring and paneling.

#1 common – This is the top quality of the regular board grades. It may have small knots and other insignificant imperfections but should have no knotholes and is a good choice for projects in which small defects are not important.

D select – This is the lowest quality of the better-grade boards.

C select – This grade may have a few small blemishes on one side, but should be almost perfect on the other. It is usually used for indoor work only, but may be used for outdoor furniture.

#1 and #2 clear – These are the best and most expensive grades. Spend the money if you wish to, but don't waste it! Use these grades only for the finest indoor and outdoor furniture.

In addition to being graded by quality, wood stock will be more or less "wet." Wetness refers to the amount of sap still left in the wood when you buy it.

Newly cut lumber is quite wet and must be air or kiln dried (seasoned) before it can be used. There is always some sap left, but it should be a very small amount. Wood that is not sufficiently dry will warp, crack, and shrink much more than dried wood. Unfortunately, there is no sure way to assess the amount of sap still left in the wood, even though the dealer may assure you it has been kiln dried. About the only hint we can give is to look at the end grain of each board (see **Figure A** again). Heartwood that is not sufficiently dry will become thinner as it loses moisture but is less likely to warp than sapwood.

When using lower grades of lumber, and consequently saving your bankroll, use your head as well. Buy a little extra so that you can eliminate the worst knots and cracks. You can repair the lumber to a certain extent by filling small cracks and gouges using exterior wood putty or a mixture of waterproof glue and sawdust. Warped boards sometimes can be weighted and straightened, but be aware that this takes time. Tap all knots to see which ones will fall out, and then glue them back in place. If a board is badly checked at the ends it's best to cut off the cracked portion, because exposure to the elements will worsen the cracks and perhaps even split the entire board. Minor checking should be filled as for cracks and gouges.

Preservatives and Finishes

Preservatives and finishes are especially important for furniture that will be exposed to the elements for extended periods of time. You probably will be less than happy to see your hard-wrought (and dearly bought) projects rot in just a few years, so take heed and don't expect that using redwood or cypress will take care of all this for you.

The two major causes of wood deterioration are decay and insect damage. Some aromatic woods are naturally insect-resistant to a degree, but the less expensive grades are less resistant than the better grades, and you probably do not want to spend the money on top-grade lumber for all the projects you build. You'll be happy to know that this problem can be solved relatively easily in these modern times, without purchasing huge pressurized vats in which to permeate the lumber with stinky old creosote.

Pentachlorophenol ("Penta" to its friends) is the primary active ingredient in some of the most common modern wood preservatives. It is available in ready-to-use form, having been diluted in an oil base. You can pour it into a bucket and soak the ends of the boards, and you can also brush it onto the surfaces of the wood. It can be painted over.

Other effective preservatives include zinc and copper naphthenates. They are odorless and may be painted over, although the copper variety leaves a pale greenish stain that will show through translucent paint. Zinc naphthenate is colorless and can be used under clear finishes.

PLEASE NOTE that these preservatives are poisonous to both plant and animal life (that includes humans). Read the labels carefully and follow all precautions for storing and using them!!

For final finishing and sealing of outdoor furnishings, synthetic varnish is your best bet. You may wish to paint some of the projects you make, but if you use any of the more attractive woods it seems a shame to cover the natural grain and color. If you do paint be certain to select exterior paint. Varnish also must be an exterior variety, preferably a marine or boat varnish. Thin the varnish for the first coat, and then use it full-strength for the second.

Adhesive

We recommend both glue and fasteners (either nails, screws, or bolts) for all joints, unless you want to be able to disassemble the project for easy storage or transport. Aliphatic resin, which is the wood glue we normally use for indoor projects, will not do for outdoor furnishings. You'll need to find a waterproof glue, and be forewarned that the term is sometimes used loosely on product labels. We suggest that you use a marine glue or a two-part epoxy that must be mixed and used immediately. Waterproof glue also may be brushed on like paint to seal end grain and prohibit water absorption. As a general rule, all glued assemblies should be clamped, but not so tightly as to force out most of the glue. Thirty minutes is sufficient clamping time for most joints. Those that will be under a great deal of stress should be clamped overnight. Joints secured with power-driven screws need not be clamped at all.

Figure B

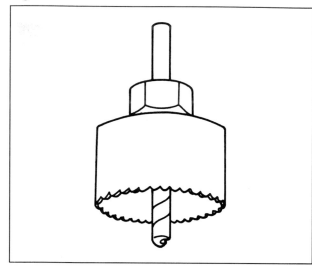

Figure D

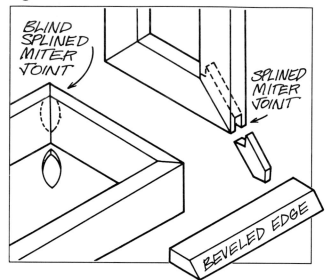

Figure C

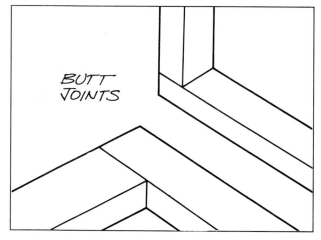

Fasteners and Other Hardware

While pure iron is quite resistant to rust, modern "iron" fasteners and hardware contain small amounts of carbon and are called "mild steel." Under outdoor (damp) conditions, mild steel eventually will rust away. More durable substances from which fasteners and hardware are made include brass, bronze, and alloyed stainless steel, although none is one-hundred percent rustproof. Your best bet will be galvanized mild-steel hardware, which is commonly available. If you can't find galvanized hardware, look for a rust-inhibiting product with which to coat steel hardware.

For a finished look, screws may be countersunk. Although this is a more common procedure for indoor furnishings and is not really necessary for more rustic outdoor projects, it will prevent the possibility of friends and family sustaining scratches caused by slightly protruding screw heads. In the same vein, finishing nails may be recessed but common nails usually are not. If you countersink the screws, the recesses may be filled with wooden plugs or wood filler. Wooden plugs will be almost invisible if you cut them from stock that matches the grain of the surrounding wood. This is easy to do, using a plug cutter (**Figure B**). Plugs also can be made by cutting slices from dowel rod, but they present end grain and will be much more apparent, particularly if the wood is stained.

Cutting and Joining

Butt Joints: A butt joint normally connects the end of one piece to the surface or edge of another (**Figure C**). The end grain of one piece will always show. Because there are no cuts made to form interlocking portions, this is an extemely weak joint. A butt joint can be strengthened using glue blocks, splines, nails, screws, dowels, or other reinforcement.

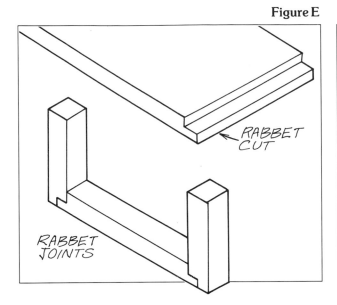

RABBET
CUT

RABBET
JOINTS

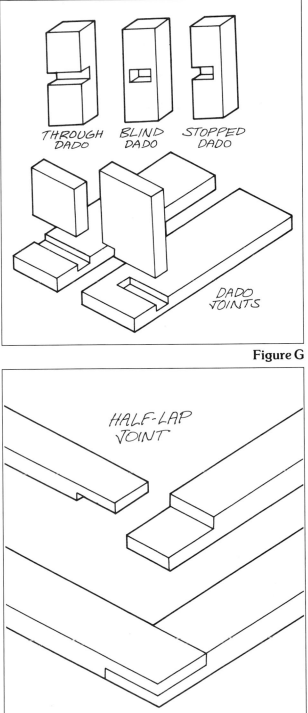

THROUGH
DADO

BLIND
DADO

STOPPED
DADO

DADO
JOINTS

HALF-LAP
JOINT

Miters and Bevels: A miter joint connects two angle-cut ends (**Figure D**). It conceals the end grain of both pieces and can be reinforced using splines, dowels, or fasteners. The most common miter is a 45-degree, which is used to construct right-angle assemblies. A bevel is an angle cut made along an edge or surface.

Rabbets: A rabbet is an L-shaped groove and has many applications. A rabbet cut into one or both pieces to be joined conceals the end grain of one piece and allows for a greater surface area to be glued, thus creating a stronger joint (**Figure E**). This joint is commonly used for cabinet sides, and for box, case, and drawer construction. Normally it is reinforced using screws or nails. A rabbet cut has other uses such as recessing the inside of a door to fit into the door opening.

Dado: Basically, a dado is a groove. Several types of dadoes and dado joints are illustrated in **Figure F**. A through dado extends all the way from edge to edge (or end to end). A stopped dado extends from one edge to a point short of the opposite edge. A blind dado is stopped short of both edges.

Lap Joints: A lap joint normally is used to connect two members at right angles. In the most common lap joint, the two joined surfaces are flush (**Figure G**). This joint provides a large area to be glued.

Mortise and Tenon Joints: There are lots of variations on this theme, but the basic garden-variety mor-

Figure H

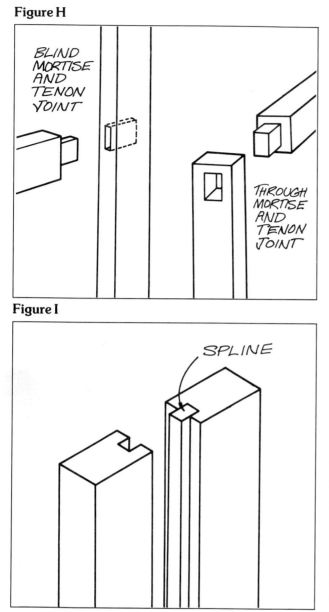

Figure I

Figure J

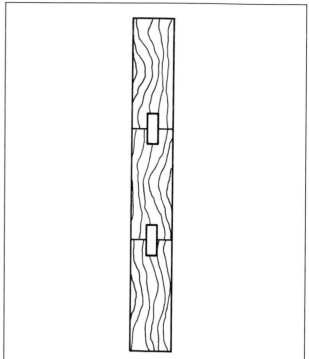

Spline Joints: A spline is a thin strip of wood used as a connecting member between two boards. It fits into dadoes cut into the edges to be joined, and can be used to strengthen any type of joint. A spline joint is shown in **Figure I**. Through splines reach from end to end. Blind splines are stopped short of the ends and cannot be seen once the joint is assembled.

Splines are specified in this book to create large parts (such as cabinet or box walls) that require several edge-joined boards to achieve the width. A splined edge joint is much stronger than one which is simply glued and clamped. Unglued splines create a structure that can expand and contract with atmospheric conditions without cracking or splitting. Unglued splines can be used, of course, only for parts that are secured at the ends to trim or other structures. In the boards that are splined together to form a wall, for instance, the splines usually may be left unglued since the wall is attached on all four edges to other structures. When edge-joining, every other board should be turned so that the ray patterns are alternated (**Figure J**) to avoid warping.

tise and tenon joints are shown in **Figure H**. This is an extremely strong joint and can be made even stronger. A pegged (or pinned) mortise and tenon joint is one in which the tenon extends out beyond the mortise and is itself mortised to accommodate a peg. The unglued, pegged mortise and tenon is a handy joint to use in furniture that you wish to disassemble for portability.

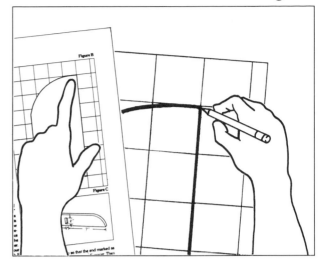

Waste Allowance

We have specified the materials required to build each project in this book. Because you cannot use every single inch of stock, especially if you purchase a lower grade of wood, we have added a waste allowance of approximately ten percent to each material called for. Special instances in which a waste allowance is not included are noted. Although it may sound like a fairly large amount, ten percent is not really a lot to allow for waste. Keep this in mind when you are at the lumberyard. We suggest that you initially purchase only enough stock to make one project, and note how much extra you have after all the parts are cut. This will give you a better basis on which to judge your purchases for subsequent projects.

Enlarging Scale Drawings

For unusually shaped or contoured parts, whenever possible we have provided full-size patterns or cutting diagrams that can be plotted directly on the wood using basic tools such as a square and angle measure. In some instances, however, we had to provide scale drawings, which are shown on a background grid of squares. Each small square on the grid is equal to a 1-inch square on the full-size part, and the drawing must be enlarged to make a full-size pattern. To enlarge a scale drawing you'll need a large piece of paper containing a grid of 1-inch squares. You can make your own pattern paper by drawing the 1-inch grid on brown wrapping paper, shelf paper, or flattened grocery bags, or you can purchase pattern paper that already contains the grid. It is available in at least two forms: as draft paper (check an art supply store) and as dressmaker's pattern paper. To enlarge the scale drawing simply copy it to the paper containing the larger grid, working one square at a time (**Figure K**).

PVC PIPE TIPS

General Characteristics

Plastic pipe is used for most plumbing jobs these days because it is virtually impervious to the elements. It is extremely strong, will not rust or decay, and is easy to cut and join using only a hand saw and special cement. These same properties make it an excellent material for furniture building.

There are several different types of plastic pipe, made according to various chemical formulas. The two strongest are PVC (polyvinyl chloride) and CPVC (chlorinated polyvinyl chloride). CPVC is the more expensive of the two.

In a way, these materials are very much like human bone. They can take a lot of straight-on pressure but will break or crack when bent too far. Extremely high temperatures will cause the pipe to soften. CPVC will remain hard at higher temperatures than PVC, but even PVC will withstand more heat (approximately 120 degrees Fahrenheit) than that to which your furniture normally will be exposed. Extremely low temperatures will not harm plastic pipe, but will make it brittle. Under freezing conditions, a sharp knock can cause the pipe to crack or shatter.

Pipe and Fittings

You will be working with straight pipe and with contoured fittings of various shapes. The fittings are used to join the straight lengths of pipe, something like a great big erector set. **Figure L** shows the most common fittings. All PVC fittings are female, fitting around rather than inside the straight pipe. As you will see when you make your first purchase, some fittings are manufactured with a "collar" at each opening and some are not. The fittings shown in **Figure L** do have collars, but it's not necessary to purchase this kind. The collars have no bearing on fit and will make no difference in the assembly of the projects. In fact, the assembly diagrams in the PVC projects in this book show fittings without collars, so you'll be able to read them more easily.

There are many more types of fittings than the ones shown here. You will find, for instance, three different types of 90-degree angle fittings. One is a standard 90-degree elbow and is the type we used. It's the one shown in **Figure L**. Another type is called a 90-degree short turn, and is shorter than the standard. A third type is called a 90-degree long sweep, and is longer than the standard. Obviously, if you use either the shorter or longer fitting in place of the standard, it will affect the size of the finished project.

There also are at least two types of double-T fittings. We used the standard double-T shown in **Figure L**, not a "cross" fitting, which is the same shape but with shorter ends. Be aware, also, that there is a difference between a standard T-fitting and what is called a double-90. They look quite similar but we used the standard T-fitting shown in **Figure L**.

Straight pipe is sized by internal diameter. A "1-inch" pipe has an inner diameter of 1 inch, give or take a little. (That's called the "tolerance.") Fitting sizes are determined by the sizes of pipe that they join, not by any measurement of the fitting itself. Thus, a fitting that accommodates 1-inch pipes is called a 1-inch fitting, even though the inner diameter of the fitting does not measure 1 inch.

Because of that little bugaboo called tolerance, and because manufacturers may vary somewhat on standard sizes, it's a good idea to test all pipe and fittings before you fork over the cash and leave the store. The pipe should slide easily into the fitting, but you should not be able to rock it up and down within the fitting. If it is too loose or too tight, simply ask for another fitting.

Pipe is graded according to its strength and normal use in various plumbing jobs. We used schedule 40 pipe and fittings for the projects in this book. If you wish to learn more about the various grades, strengths, and uses, consult your plumbing supply dealer.

Figure L

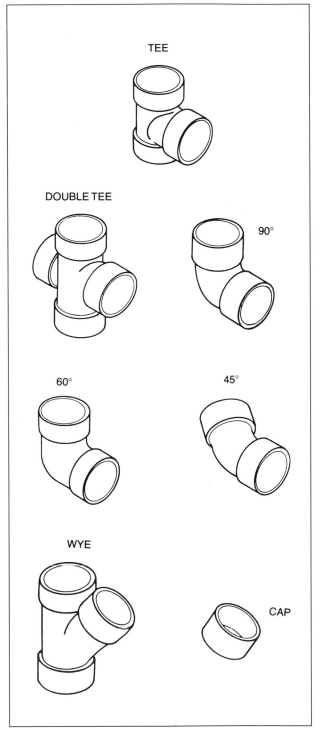

BUILDING OUTDOOR FURNITURE

Securing the Joints

When PVC is used for plumbing, the joints are sealed with a special solvent cement that sets off a chemical reaction, permanently welding the pipe and fittings. For furniture, you have the option of securing the joints with self-tapping screws, allowing you to disassemble the structure if and when you want to.

If you opt for cemented joints, be sure to purchase the particular solvent cement made for use with the type of pipe you buy. Even within this limitation, you will have a choice of cements, each with a different set-up time. The one with the longest set-up time is the easiest to use, because it allows an extra minute or two for adjustments before the joint is locked for all eternity.

And we do mean all eternity. There is no way to disassemble a cemented joint short of sawing off the pipe and starting over again with new pieces. You should dry assemble each project to make sure that all parts fit together properly before cementing any joint. You may have to trim some of the pieces slightly, but be sure that all pieces are inserted into the fittings as far as they will go before you decide they need trimming.

If you use cement, read the manufacturer's instructions carefully. Most require that you clean both the pipe and the fitting, then assemble the joint and give the pipe a twist to force out air bubbles. Work in a well-ventilated area, as the fumes are noxious to say the least!

If you want to be able to disassemble the project, do not use cement. Instead, secure each joint with two self-tapping screws. Pre-drill the screw holes, using a bit slightly smaller than the diameter of the screw shank. It's a good idea to mark each corresponding pipe and fitting with a code letter, to facilitate reassembly.

Cutting and Drilling

Straight PVC pipe is sold in standard lengths. You'll have to cut the pipe into the shorter pieces specified for each project. There are no special tricks to cutting the pipe; just mark off the lengths and cut in as straight a line as possible, so the pipe will fit squarely into the fitting. If you wrap a straight piece of paper around the pipe at the point you wish to cut, and tape the paper in place, you can follow the edge with your saw to get a nice square cut (**Figure M**).

We suggest that you mark off all of the required

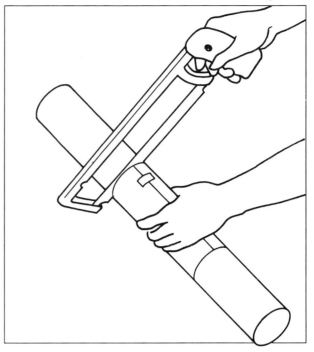

Figure M

lengths, starting with the longest ones, before you begin to cut. There will be much less waste this way. File off any burrs or rough spots on the cut ends. For the PVC projects in this book, we have added a waste allowance to the specified materials, as we did for the wood.

You can use any type of saw with a fine-toothed blade to cut plastic pipe. A hack saw will work just fine. If you have access to a band saw, it will speed the cutting process. There is a gadget called a ratchet shear (**Figure N**) that is made especially for cutting plastic pipe. It works much like scissors. We tested it, and it seems to work well, but we prefer the band saw.

The PVC projects in this book occasionally require you to drill holes in the pipe and/or fittings. Again, there are no special tricks. You can use a hand-held power drill with a normal metal or wood bit. For large holes, use a spade bit with your hand-held drill (**Figure O**), or use a plug cutter.

Please take special note of the following tip. We have specified the diameter of each hole to be drilled, but you will find that those specified diameters are not generally correct. Here's why: As we said before, pipe

Figure N

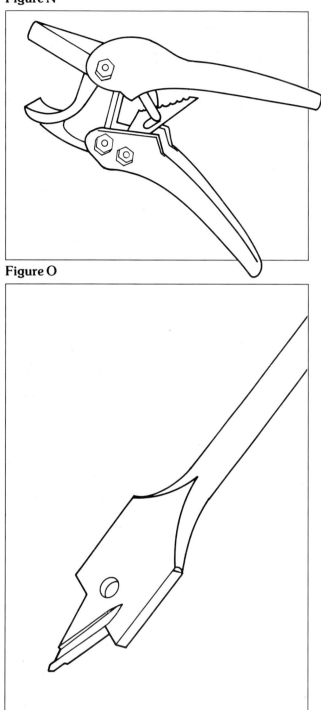

Figure O

is sized by internal diameter. While the internal diameter of all 1-inch pipe will always measure very close to 1 inch, the external diameter will vary greatly from brand to brand and from grade to grade. Some pipe simply has thicker walls. So, you can see that while one type of 1-inch pipe might have an external diameter of 1¼ inches, another type might measure 1½ inches. In order to eliminate a lot of excess verbiage when specifying the diameters of the holes you need to drill, we have always called for a hole the same size or slightly larger than the INTERNAL diameter of the pipe to be inserted in the hole. You can drill the holes to the sizes specified and then enlarge them using a drill or file, or you can measure the EXTERNAL diameter of the pipe that will be inserted into the hole and drill the hole to that size.

Finishing

PVC pipe and fittings are manufactured for general use in four colors: beige, white, gray, and black. If you prefer a different color, just add paint. Almost any type of paint will work but oil-based paint is best. There are paints make especially for use with plastic pipe. Whatever type of paint you use, spraying gives a smoother look than brushing.

It is important to prepare the surface before painting. First, clean the pipe using turpentine or PVC cleaner to remove dirt and oily residues. Add a coat of primer, allow it to dry, and then paint. Two thin coats of paint will stand up better than one thick one. We suggest that you assemble the project before you do any surface preparation or painting.

If you opt not to paint, you'll have to decide how to treat the printed information (manufacturer's name, size, etc.) that appears on many brands of pipe and fittings. You can sometimes turn the pieces so that the printing is hidden on the assembled project, or you might want to display it prominently for a funky look. Then again, you may wish to do away with it entirely. The printing can be taken off using acetone, fingernail polish remover, automotive choke cleaner, or paint remover. Pour the liquid on a clean rag and rub along the printing in one direction only, so you do not smear the ink all over the pipe.

Glider Swing

This old-fashioned glider swing will serve as either a freestanding glider suspended in its own base, or a swing, used without the base and suspended by chains from your porch ceiling or a friendly old tree. The base is 5 feet long, 2 feet tall, and 2½ feet deep, with a handy drinking-glass holder cut into each armrest. The swing is 4 feet long, 2 feet tall, and nearly that deep.

Materials

For the base:

Note: If you plan to use this project as a swing and not as a glider, you need not build the base.

40 linear feet of 1 x 4 oak

Two 5-foot lengths of 1 x 3 oak (No waste allowance has been included for the 1 x 3, so you may wish to purchase 6-foot lengths if the ends are split.)

Four heavy-duty eye bolts, each 2¾ inches long

Twenty-eight No. 6 gauge flathead wood screws, each 1½ inches long; and a few 2d finishing nails

For the swing:

17 linear feet of 1 x 3 oak

Eight oak 1 x 2s, each 8 feet long (No waste allowance has been included, so you may wish to purchase 9- or 10- foot lengths if the ends are not perfect.)

Four heavy-duty eye bolts, each 3¼ inches long

Fifty No. 6 gauge flathead wood screws, each 1½ inches long

Chain: If you plan to suspend the swing from its own base as a glider, you'll need a 2-foot length of chain. If you plan to use it as a swing, the amount of chain you'll need will depend on the height of the porch ceiling or tree branch. In that case, for each side of the swing figure on a single length of chain to reach from the ceiling or branch down to a few inches above the the armrest, plus another 3 feet to form the inverted "V" that joins the end of the suspension chain to the two eye bolts. Many hardware and home improvement centers carry packaged porch swing chain that's already assembled in the proper configuration, and all you have to do is cut it to length. Whatever approach you choose, be certain that the chain you select is rated to hold a sufficient weight. In addition, be certain that the hardware that will serve to connect the chain to the ceiling or tree branch is of the proper type and sufficient strength to hold the weight.

The glider is made in two separate parts: the base and the swing. The base is a freestanding structure from which the swing hangs by four short chains. The swing can be used as is, or you may wish to add cushions.

THE BASE

The freestanding base consists of two identical end sections and three connecting braces. Because the braces are joined to the end sections using pegged mortise and tenon joints, the base can be disassembled quite easily for storage or transport.

Cutting the Parts

1. Overall dimensions of all parts required to build the base are listed below. Some of the parts will be shaped or otherwise altered after they are cut, according to the instructions provided in later steps. For now, cut the parts as specified here and label each with its identifying code.

Code	Length	Quantity	Material
A	24 inches	2	1 x 4
B	24 inches	4	1 x 4
C	30 inches	4	1 x 4
D	11 inches	2	1 x 4
E	4 inches	2	1 x 4
F	8 inches	2	1 x 4
G	26 inches	2	1 x 4
H	62 inches	1	1 x 4
I	3 inches	2	1 x 4
J	2½ inches	1	1 x 4
K	2½ inches	1	1 x 4
L	60 inches	2	1 x 3

2. The B pieces will serve as vertical supports for the armrests as shown in the assembly diagram, **Figure L**. Each of the B pieces must be mortised to accommodate a brace that joins the two end sections. Cut a mortise through each B piece, following the dimensions provided in **Figure A**. The mortise should be centered between the long edges of the piece, but note that it is closer to one end than the other. We suggest that you mark the end specified as the top for later reference.

3. The C pieces will serve as feet on each end section as shown in **Figure J**. Each must be mortised to accommodate a brace and rounded off at the two upper corners. A scale drawing for the corner contour is provided in **Figure B**. Enlarge the drawing and transfer the curved outline to both ends of each C piece. The

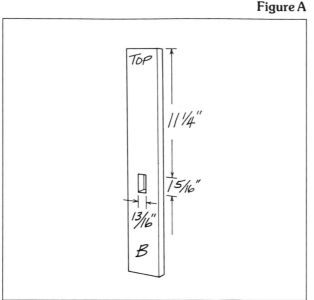

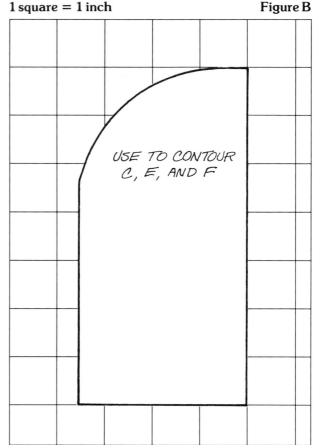

USE TO CONTOUR
C, E, AND F

straight lower edge of the piece should still be 30 inches long when you have finished cutting the contours on the upper corners.

4. Cut a mortise through each contoured C piece, following the dimensions provided in **Figure C**. The mortise should be equally distant from the upper and lower edges, but note that it is closer to the front end than to the back. We suggest that you mark the end designated as the front for later reference.

5. The foot assembly of each end section is a sort of sandwich, if you will. Two C pieces are the "bread," and the "filling" consists of three spacers and the ends of the vertical B pieces. To get a clearer picture of this refer to **Figures I** and **J**, which show an exposed view of the filling layer and the completed foot sandwich respectively. As you can see, in the filling layer a D piece serves as the center spacer, an E piece serves as the front spacer, and an F piece serves as the back spacer. Use the pattern you made from **Figure B** to contour one corner of each E piece and one corner of each F piece, being careful not to shorten the straight lower edge of any of the pieces.

6. The center spacers (D pieces) must be mortised to match the outer C pieces. The best way to get a perfect match is to align the pieces that form the filling layer as shown in **Figure I**, and place a C piece on top, being

Figure C

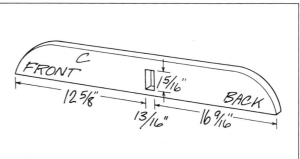

certain to place the C piece so that the end marked as the front is aligned with the shorter front E spacer. Then simply trace around the edge of the mortise that you already cut in the C piece to transfer the outline to the D piece below it. Use this procedure to trace the mortise outline onto each D piece, and cut the mortises.

Figure D   **1 square = 1 inch**

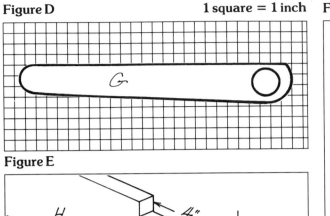

Figure E

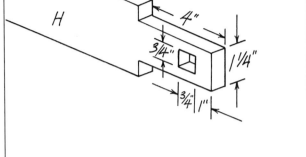

Figure F

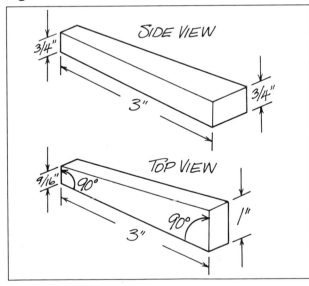

Figure G

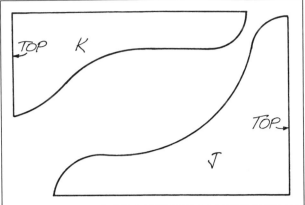

7. The G pieces will serve as the armrests. A scale drawing of the armrest is provided in **Figure D**. Enlarge the drawing to make a full-size pattern, and cut the contours on each G piece.

8. We created a recessed drinking-glass holder in each armrest to help prevent spilled refreshments when the swinging gets rambunctious. Placement of the circular holder is shown on the scale drawing. The easiest way to cut this is to use a plug or circle cutter to completely remove a 2½-inch-diameter circle from the armrest where indicated. Cut a ¼-inch-thick slice from the circle and glue it back into the hole, flush with the bottom. You'll probably need to use some wood filler around the edge, since it will be slightly smaller than the hole. Note that the two armrests should be mirror images of each other, so glue the circular cutouts flush with opposite surfaces of the two armrests.

9. The H piece will serve as the lower brace that connects the two end sections, and requires a tenon at each end. In addition, the tenons must be mortised to accommodate the pegs. Refer to **Figure E** as you cut a tenon at each end of the H piece, and cut a mortise through each tenon as shown.

10. The six required pegs are cut from the two I pieces. Begin by cutting three 1 x 3-inch blocks from each I piece. Taper each block to form a peg, as shown in the top and side view drawings, **Figure F**.

11. Each armrest is supported in part by two small decorative blocks – one near the front and one near the back – as shown in **Figures L** and **M**. Full-size patterns for the front and back blocks are provided in **Figure G**. Cut two front blocks from the J piece and two back blocks from the K piece. Label the front blocks J and the back blocks K.

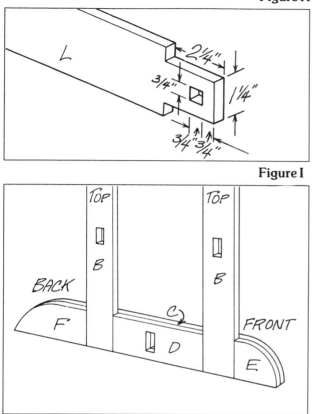

Figure I

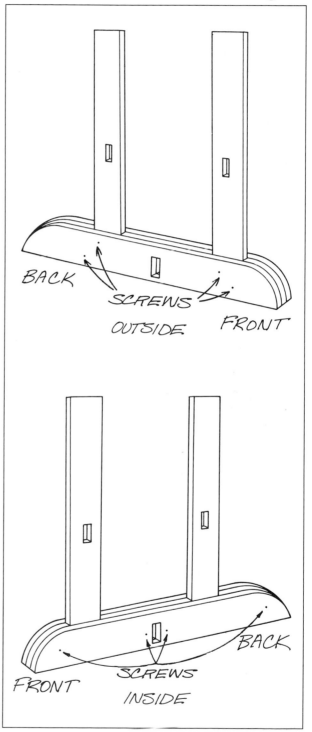

12. Each of the L pieces will serve as an upper brace between the two end sections. They require mortised tenons similar to the ones you cut at the ends of the H piece. Refer to **Figure H** for exact dimensions.

Assembly

1. Begin assembling one end section by making one of the foot sandwiches we talked about earlier. Place one of the C pieces on a flat surface and arrange on top of it the pieces that form the filling layer of the sandwich, as shown in **Figure I**. Be certain to turn each B piece so that the end you marked as the top is indeed at the top, and not sandwiched between the spacers at the bottom. Place a second C piece on top of the filling layer and check to be sure that the mortises in both C pieces and the center D piece all are aligned. If they are not, you may have one or both of the C pieces turned the wrong way end for end. Secure the assembly using

Figure K

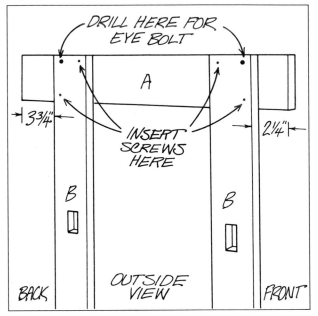

DRILL HERE FOR EYE BOLT

A

3¾"

INSERT SCREWS HERE

B   B

2¼"

BACK   OUTSIDE VIEW   FRONT

eight screws: four inserted from one side and four from the other. Suggested placement of the screws is shown in **Figure J**. The four screws inserted from the outside will hold the spacers in place, and the four inserted from the inside will hold the legs in place.

2. Add a horizontal **A** piece on the inside, flush with the tops of the legs as shown in **Figure K**. Secure each joint with two screws inserted through the leg and into the **A** piece as shown, allowing at least 1½ inches horizontal distance between the screws. Drill a 5/16-inch-diameter hole through each leg and on through the **A** piece where indicated, to accommodate an eye bolt. We drilled a shallow socket on the outside of each hole so the nuts could be countersunk. Insert an eye bolt through each hole from the inside, and install the nut.

3. Glue a contoured **J** piece to the outside of the front leg, centered between the side edges and flush with the upper edge (**Figure L**). Glue a **K** piece to the back leg in the same manner and secure each decorative block

Figure L

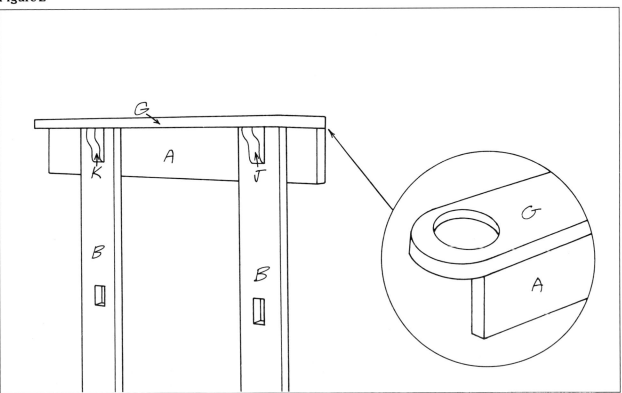

G

K   A   J

B   B

G

A

BUILDING OUTDOOR FURNITURE

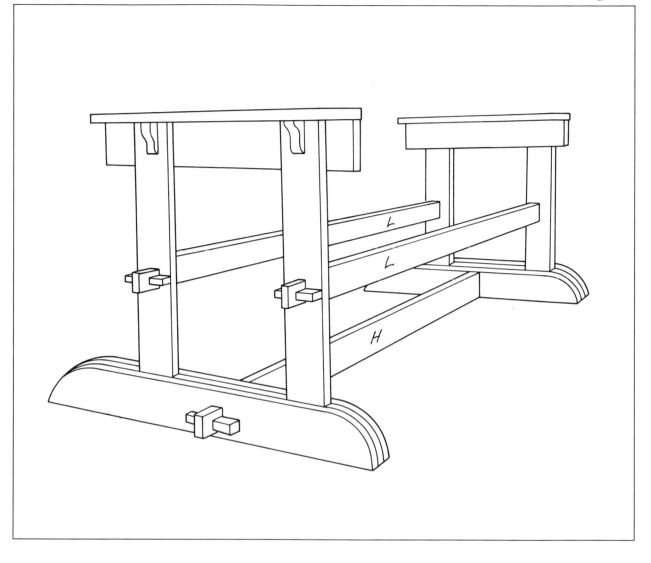

with a single finishing nail. Place the armrest (**G**) on top of the **A**, **B**, **J**, and **K** pieces so that the long straight edge is flush with the inside surface of the **A** piece (**Figure L**). The armrest should extend just slightly beyond the **A** piece at the front, and an inch or so beyond it at the back. Secure the armrest using two screws inserted down into the **A** piece.

4. Repeat the procedures in steps 1 through 3 to create a second end section. Note that it should be a mirror image of the first one.

5. Align the two end sections about 6 feet apart, with the inside of each section facing what will be the center of the glider base. Place the **H** piece and the two **L** pieces lengthwise between them. Insert one end of the **H** piece through the mortise in the foot assembly of one end section. Insert one end of each **L** piece through the mortise in one leg of the same end section. Insert the opposite ends of the braces through the corresponding mortises of the opposite end section, and secure all joints with pegs as shown in **Figure M**.

Figure N 1 square = 1 inch

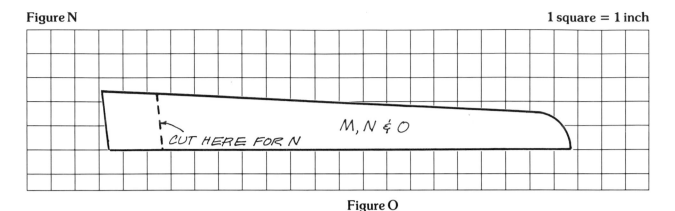

CUT HERE FOR N

M, N & O

THE SWING

The swing itself is quite simple, consisting of two identical end sections connected by sixteen slats.

Cutting the Parts

1. Overall dimensions of all parts required to build the swing are listed below. Some will be shaped or altered after they are cut, according to the instructions provided in later steps. For now, cut the parts as specified here and label each with its identifying code.

Code	Length	Quantity	Material
M	20½ inches	2	1 x 3
N	18 inches	2	1 x 3
O	20½ inches	2	1 x 3
P	19 inches	2	1 x 3
Q	12¾ inches	2	1 x 3
R	48 inches	16	1 x 2

2. Each M piece will serve as a vertical back support for one of the end sections (**Figure R**). A scale drawing for the contoured M piece is provided in **Figure N**. Enlarge the drawing to make a full-size pattern and cut the contour on each M piece.

3. Each N piece will serve as a horizontal seat support for one of the end sections (**Figure R**), and each O piece will serve as an inner seat support. These pieces are identical to the M piece. Use the pattern you made for the M piece to cut the contours on the O and N pieces, making the N pieces shorter as noted on the scale drawing.

Figure O

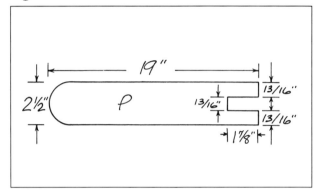

Figure P

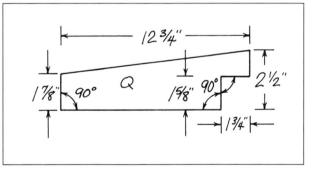

4. Each P piece will serve as an armrest for one end section, and is rounded off at the front and grooved at the back to fit around the M piece. A cutting diagram for the armrest is provided in **Figure O**. Follow the diagram to modify the two P pieces.

5. Each Q piece will serve as an armrest support for one end section, and is tapered and notched as shown in the cutting diagram, **Figure P**. Modify each Q piece as shown.

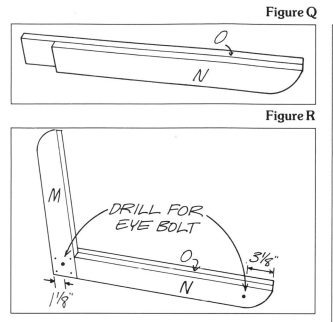

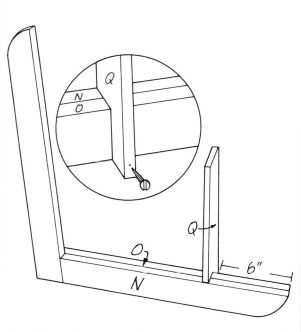

Assembly

1. To begin assembling one end section, place an **N** and an **O** piece together to form the seat support as shown in **Figure Q**. Secure the assembly using two screws inserted through the **O** piece and into the **N** piece. For future reference, the **O** piece is on the inside of the end section, that is, it faces what will be the center of the swing.

2. Add an **M** piece to this assembly to form the back support (**Figure R**). Note that the pieces do not form a right angle, but rather a slightly wider angle. Secure the **M** piece using four screws inserted through it and into the **O** piece. Drill two ⁵⁄₁₆-inch-diameter holes where indicated to accommodate the eye bolts.

3. Glue the armrest support (**Q**) in place 6 inches from the front ends of the **N** and **O** pieces as shown in **Figure S**. Secure it by inserting a single screw through the lower extension of the **Q** piece, into the **O** piece.

4. Add the armrest (**P**) as shown in **Figure T**. The back grooved end fits around the upright **M** piece. Secure the armrest using one screw at the front inserted down through the armrest into the support (**Q**), and one screw at the back inserted from the inside, through the armrest into the **M** piece.

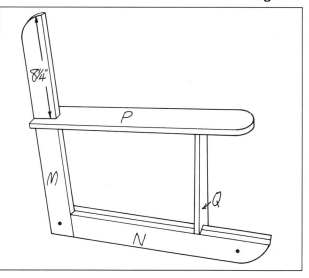

5. Install an eye bolt in each of the drilled holes, inserting it from the outside in. Secure each bolt with a washer and nut. There's no need to countersink the nuts, since they will be out of harm's way underneath and facing the inside of the swing.

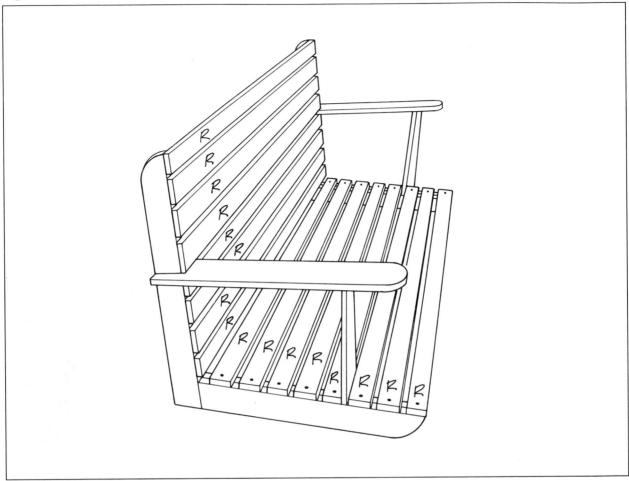

6. Repeat the procedures in steps 1 through 5 to create a second end section, making it a mirror image of the first one.

7. The R pieces will serve as slats that form the seat and back (**Figure U**). Align the two end sections about 4 feet apart and place one slat on top of them at the front. The front edge of the slat should be even with the front of each seat support, and each end of the slat should be even with the outer surface of the seat support. Secure the slat at each end using a single screw inserted down through the slat into the seat support. Attach a second seat slat in the same manner, allowing a ¾-inch space between the two slats. The third seat slat should butt against the front of the armrest support (Q

piece) on each end section, and the fourth should butt against the back of the support. Continue to add seat slats, allowing a ¾-inch space between. There are eight seat slats in all.

8. The eight remaining R pieces will serve as the back slats. Attach them to the upright M pieces (back supports) of the end sections in the same manner.

Final Assembly

To assemble the glider, cut the 2-foot chain into four lengths to hang the swing from the frame. Alternately, use the longer chain assemblies to hang the swing from a porch or tree.

Square Chair

Straight, clean lines and simple construction make this a very popular project, along with its companion pieces – the parson's table and coffee table. We think this set is classy enough to serve as either indoor or outdoor furniture, especially when made from one of the beautiful hardwoods such as pecan. The chair is approximately 20 inches square and 32 inches tall.

Materials

40 linear feet of 1 x 3 pecan

3 linear feet of ¾ x ¾-inch pecan or other wooden stripping

Fasteners: If you peg the joints you'll need 12 feet of ⅜-inch-diameter wooden dowel rod from which to cut sixteen 4-inch-long pegs and thirty-two 2-inch-long pegs. (Or, purchase pegs already cut.) You'll also need eight No. 6 gauge flathead wood screws, each 1¼ inches long, with which to attach the support strips. If you choose not to peg the joints you'll need sixteen No. 18 gauge flathead wood screws, each 3½ inches long; and thirty-two No. 6 gauge flathead wood screws, each 1½ inches long; in addition to the slightly shorter screws already specified.

The square chair is constructed in four separate sections: two identical sides, the back, and the seat. For each section the parts are simply cut to length and assembled using butt joints secured with pegs or screws.

Cutting the Parts

1. Cut the parts listed below from 1 x 3 pecan and label each with its identifying code.

Code	Length	Quantity
A	14 inches	4
B	25 inches	4
C	12 inches	2
D	13¾ inches	4
E	18¾ inches	2
F	17¼ inches	7
G	18 inches	2

2. Cut two 17¼-inch lengths of ¾ x ¾-inch stripping. These will serve as the support strips.

Building the Sections

1. One complete side section is shown in **Figure A**. The upper A piece serves as the armrest and the B pieces serve as the legs. Assemble one side section, butting the pieces as shown, and secure the joints using long pegs or long screws inserted through the legs into the ends of the A pieces. Assemble a second identical

Figure A

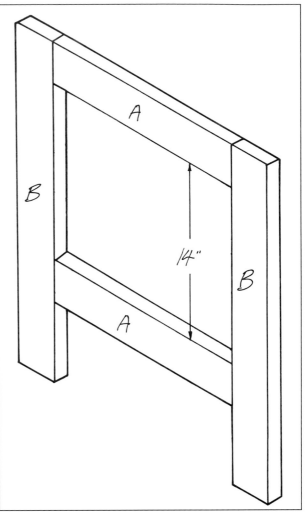

side section in the same manner. (Note: When pegging a joint, glue and clamp the joint and allow the glue to dry. Then drill a ⅜-inch-diameter peg hole, spread glue on the peg, and insert it into the hole. Trim the end of the peg flush with the wood.)

2. The back section is shown in **Figure B**. Glue the four slats (D) between the vertical C pieces, allowing approximately ¾ inch of space between slats. The upper and lower slats should be flush with the ends of the C pieces. Secure each slat using one of the long screws or long pegs inserted through the C piece into each end of the slat.

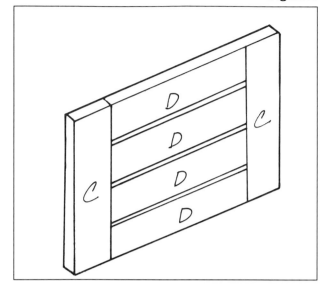

Figure C

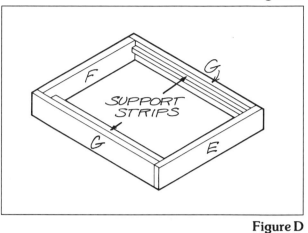

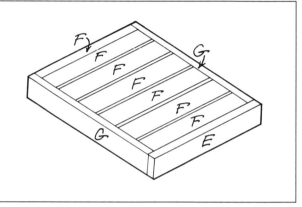

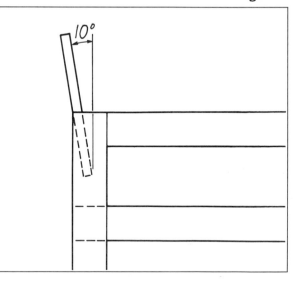

3. The seat consists of slats contained within a frame. Assemble the frame as shown in **Figure C**, using an E piece as the front member, an **F** piece as the back member, and **G** pieces as the sides. Note that the front E piece covers the ends of the G pieces but the G pieces cover the ends of the back F piece. Glue a support strip along the inside of each G piece, ¾ inch down from the upper edge. Secure the frame joints using 2-inch pegs or 1½-inch screws. Secure each support strip using four 1¼-inch screws.

4. Use the six remaining F pieces as the seat slats (**Figure D**). Place them inside the frame, with the ends resting on the support strips and allowing approximately ½ inch of space between slats. The front and back slats should be flush against the front and back frame members. Secure the slats using 2-inch pegs or 1½-inch screws inserted through the frame members into the ends of the slats.

Assembly

The assembled chair is shown in **Figure F**. Use the remaining E piece as a lower brace between the two side sections. Glue the seat and back sections between the sides, tilting the back section as shown in **Figure E** for greater comfort. Use the remaining pegs or screws to secure the assembled sections.

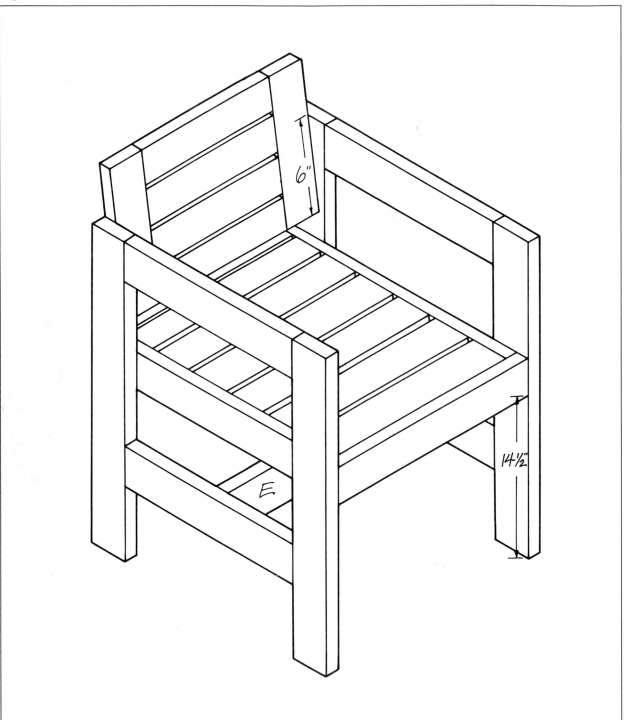

Parson's Table

This simple table is a real breeze to build and is designed to complement the square chair and coffee table. We pegged the joints but you may prefer to use wood screws. The parson's table is 19 inches square and 18 inches tall.

Figure A

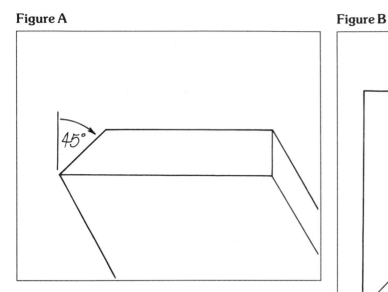

Figure B

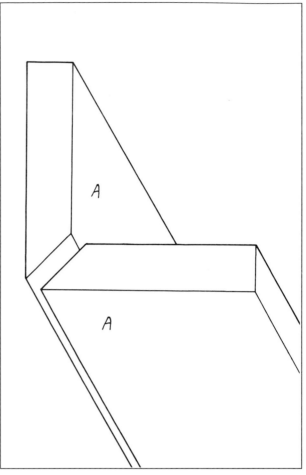

Materials

30 linear feet of 1 x 3 pecan

Fasteners: If you peg the joints you'll need 5 linear feet of ⅜-inch-diameter wooden dowel rod, from which to cut twenty-two 2-inch-long pegs and four 1¾-inch-long pegs. (Or, you may purchase pegs already cut.) You'll also need eight No. 6 gauge flathead wood screws, each 1¼ inches long, with which to secure the support blocks. If you choose not to peg the joints you'll need twenty-six No. 6 gauge flathead wood screws, each 1½ inches long; in addition to the slightly shorter screws already specified.

The parson's table consists of seven tabletop slats contained within a frame that is formed by the four legs and four horizontal spacers. Each leg consists of two vertical boards joined together at right angles.

Cutting the Parts

1. Cut the parts listed below and label each with its identifying code.

Code	Length	Quantity
A	18 inches	8
B	14 inches	4
C	2½ inches	4
D	17½ inches	7

2. The **A** pieces will serve as the legs. They are beveled to fit together in pairs as shown in **Figure A**. Cut a 45-degree bevel along one long edge of each **A** piece.

Assembly

1. Begin by joining the **A** pieces in pairs to form the legs. Glue each pair together as shown in **Figure B**, and secure each leg using a shorter peg or longer screw near one end of the assembly. This will be the lower end of the leg. The upper end will be secured later. (Note: When pegging a joint, glue and clamp the joint and allow the glue to dry. Then drill a ⅜-inch-diameter peg hole, spread glue on the peg, and insert it into the hole. Trim the end of the peg flush with the wood.)

Figure C

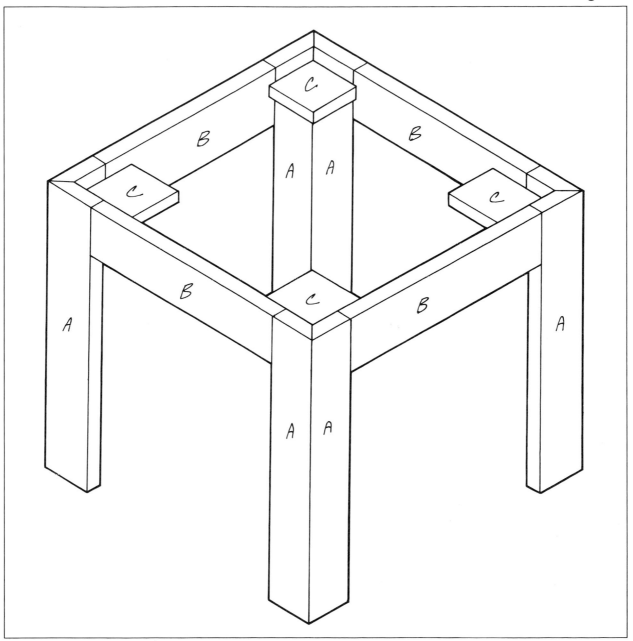

2. Now glue together the assembled legs and the B spacers to form the table frame as shown in **Figure C**. All edges should be flush at the top. Glue a square C piece into each corner as a support block, recessing the blocks ¾ inch down from the upper edges of the legs and spacers, and secure each block using two of the shorter wood screws. Insert the screws through the C blocks at an angle, into the B spacers.

Figure D

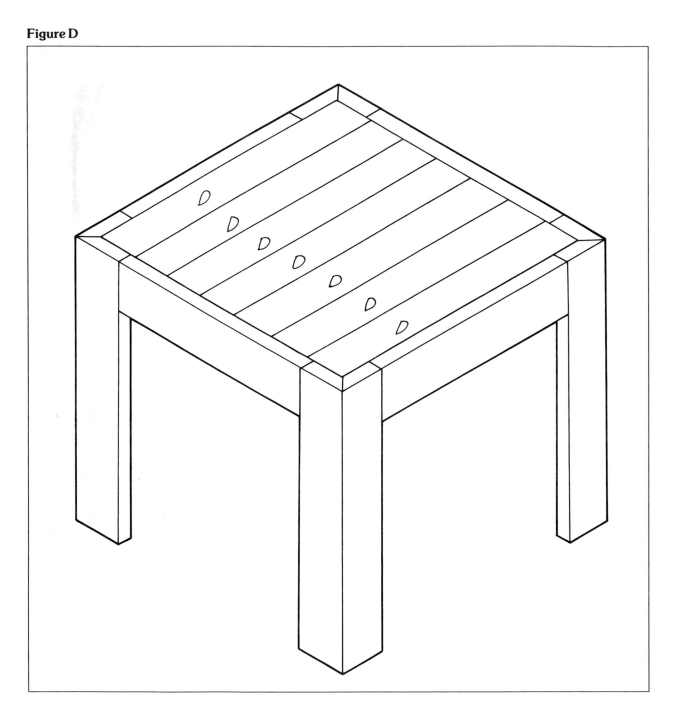

3. The D pieces will serve as the tabletop slats. Glue them inside the frame as shown in **Figure D**. Secure each slat using either pegs or screws inserted through the legs or B pieces. If you use screws, countersink them and cut plugs to fill the holes. If you use pegs, simply trim them flush with the surface.

Coffee Table

Like its companion pieces, the parson's table and square chair, this project is very easy to build yet looks distinctive. The boards are simply cut to length and assembled using butt joints secured with pegs or screws. Because of the straightforward construction, overall dimensions of any of these pieces can be altered easily. We made the coffee table roughly 40 x 20 x 18 inches.

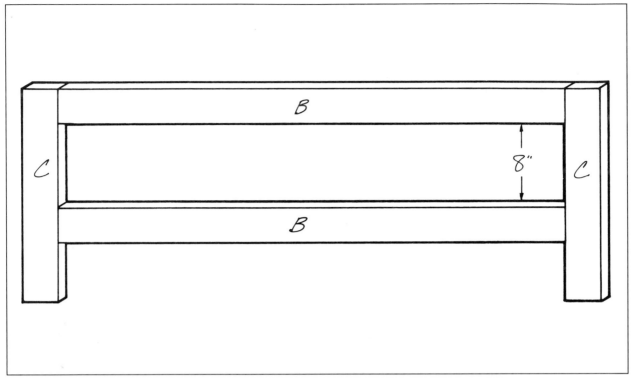

Materials

50 linear feet of 1 x 3 pecan

7 linear feet of ¾ x ¾-inch pecan or other wooden stripping

Fasteners: If you peg the joints you'll need 12 linear feet of ⅜-inch-diameter wooden dowel rod, from which to cut forty-four 2-inch-long pegs and eight 4-inch-long pegs. (Or purchase pegs already cut.) You'll also need twelve No. 6 gauge flathead wood screws, each 1¼ inches long with which to secure the support strips. If you do not peg the joints, you'll need forty-four No. 6 gauge flathead wood screws, each 1½ inches long; and eight No. 18 gauge flathead wood screws, each 3½ inches long; in addition to the slightly shorter screws already specified.

The coffee table consists of two identical side frame sections joined by three cross frame pieces. The tabletop slats fit inside the frame and rest on support strips attached along the inside of the frame.

Cutting the Parts

1. Cut the following parts from 1 x 3 pecan and label each with its identifying code.

Code	Length	Quantity
A	17 inches	19
B	36¼ inches	4
C	18 inches	4

2. Cut two 39¾-inch lengths of ¾ x ¾-inch stripping. These will be the support strips.

Assembly

1. Glue together one side frame section as shown in **Figure A**, using two B and two C pieces. The C pieces will serve as the legs. Secure each end of the lower B piece only using two of the longer pegs or two of the longer screws inserted through the leg and into the end of the B piece. Do not secure the ends of the upper B piece. They will be secured later to the cross-

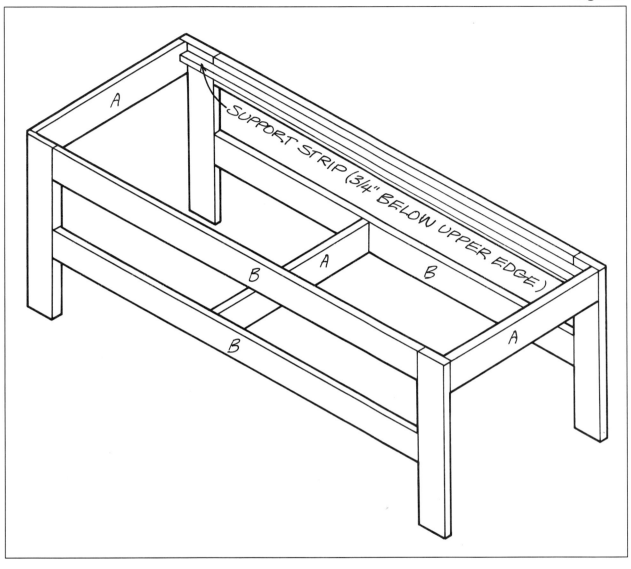

frame pieces. Build an identical side frame section using the remaining B and C pieces. (Note: When pegging a joint, glue and clamp the joint and allow the glue to dry. Then drill a 3/8-inch-diameter peg hole, spread glue on the peg, and insert it into the hole. Trim the peg flush with the wood.)

2. Join the two side frame sections using three A pieces as shown in **Figure B**. One A piece serves as a lower brace between the two frame sections, midway between the ends of the B piece on each side. The remaining two A pieces serve as upper frame ends and should be attached between the two side sections, flush with the upper edges as shown. Secure the lower A brace by inserting two of the shorter pegs or two of the 1½-inch screws through the B piece into each end. Secure each upper A piece by inserting two of the shorter pegs or two of the 1½-inch screws through the leg into each end.

Figure C

3. Glue one support strip along the inside of each upper **B** piece, ¾ inch down from the upper edge as shown in **Figure B**. Secure each support strip with six of the shortest screws.

4. The remaining sixteen **A** pieces will serve as the tabletop slats. Glue them inside the frame as shown in **Figure C**, with the ends resting on the support strips and no spaces between slats. Secure each slat by inserting one peg or screw through the frame into the end of the slat.

Sling Chair

We've renamed this one the "Ahhhhhh Chair," because everyone says that when they first sit down. The only problem you'll have will be ousting visitors who are too comfortable to move. Overall dimensions are 28 x 33 x 42 inches.

Figure A

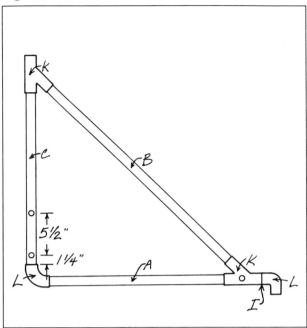

Materials

For the frame:
34 feet of straight 1½-inch PVC pipe
1½-inch PVC fittings: fourteen 90-degree angle joints, six Y-joints, and two T-joints
11 feet of straight ¾-inch CPVC pipe
¾-inch CPVC fittings: four end caps, and one double-T joint (We didn't have a double-T in this size, so we made one from a regular T-joint and an end cap.)
PVC solvent cement, or about 100 No. 6 gauge self-tapping sheet metal screws, each 1 inch long
CPVC solvent cement
Six hex-head machine bolts, each 4 inches long and ⅜ inch in diameter with a cap nut to fit

For the sling:
3 yards of heavy canvas fabric, at least 40 inches wide
Thread to match the fabric
One standard chaise lounge cushion

There are two separate assemblies that form the frame: the seat assembly and the arm assembly. The seat assembly consists of five sections: two identical side sections (**Figure A**), identical back and front sections (**Figure B**), and a criss-cross brace section that is shown on the completed seat assembly in **Figure C**. The arm assembly consists of four sections: two identical armrest sections (**Figure D**), a back support section (**Figure E**), and a front section that is identical to the front and back sections of the seat assembly. The completed arm assembly is shown in **Figure F**. In the final step, the arm and seat assemblies are bolted together as shown in **Figure G**.

Cutting the Pipe

1. The lengths of 1½-inch pipe listed below were calculated on the basis of ¾-inch fitting allowances. Check the depth of each 1½-inch fitting and recalculate each length, if necessary, to compensate for the difference on each end. Cut and label the lengths of straight pipe. Label each fitting with the code letter listed.

Code	Length	Quantity
A	25 inches	2
B	35⅜ inches	2
C	24⅛ inches	2
D	20½ inches	2
E	21½ inches	2
F	5⅜ inches	4
G	23½ inches	2
H	36¼ inches	2
I	1⅜ inches	6
Fittings:		
J	T-joint	
K	Y-joint	
L	90-degree joint	
M	End cap	

2. Cut and label the lengths of ¾-inch pipe listed below. There's no need to recalculate for fitting allowances. Label the fittings as listed.

Code	Length	Quantity
N	26 inches	2
O	17 inches	4
Fittings:		
P	End cap	
Q	Double T-joint	

Building the Seat Assembly

1. Assemble one side section as shown in **Figure A**. Use a short I piece to connect the K and L fittings shown on the lower right-hand portion of the drawing.

2. The side section is drilled in two places to accommodate the rods that will hold the fabric sling in place. Drill a ¾-inch-diameter hole through the lower K fitting where indicated, in one side and out the other. Drill in as straight a line as possible, or you'll be sorry when you try to insert the rod. Drill another ¾-inch hole through the vertical C piece, 1¼ inches above the fitting. Again, drill in one side and out the other in as straight a line as possible.

3. The side section is also drilled to accommodate the criss-cross brace section. Drill a ¾-inch hole into the C piece, 5½ inches above the lower hole that you just drilled (**Figure A**). Drill through one side of the pipe only. The brace pipe will be inserted at an angle, so enlarge the hole lengthwise until it measures about 1⅜ inches from top to bottom.

4. Repeat the procedures in steps 1, 2, and 3 to form an identical side section. Be extremely careful to align the holes you drill with the ones in the first section.

5. Assemble the front section as shown in **Figure B**.

6. Assemble an identical back section (**Figure B**).

7. The back section only must be drilled to accommodate the upper ends of the criss-cross brace section. Drill a ¾-inch hole into each L fitting, in the exact center of the inside corner angle. Do not drill all the way through the fitting and out the other side.

8. The sections that you have built are joined together with the criss-cross braces to form the seat assembly (**Figure C**). First, assemble the braces by inserting the four O pieces into the openings of the Q fitting. To begin the seat assembly, place the two triangular side sections side by side, with the elongated holes facing center. Insert the criss-cross brace as shown. Insert a short I piece into the open fitting at the top of each side section, and install the back section on top. If the brace section is too long or too wide to allow the back section to fit properly, trim the straight braces, a little at a time so you don't overcompensate. Finally, insert a short I piece into the L fitting at each end of the front section, and install the section as shown.

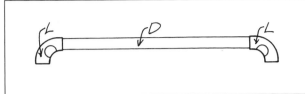

Figure C

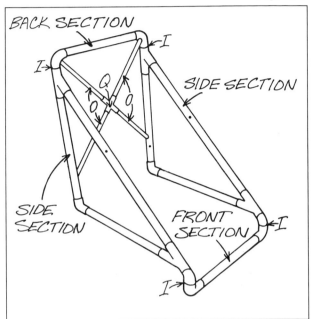

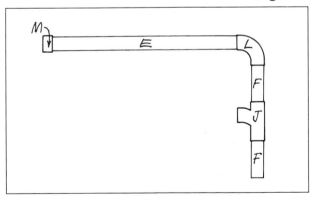

Building the Arm Assembly

1. Assemble one armrest section (**Figure D**).

2. Assemble an identical armrest section.

Figure E

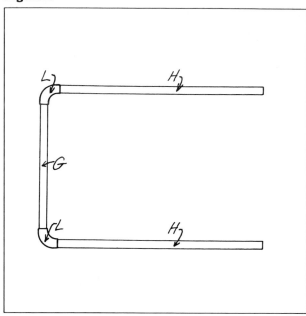

Figure F

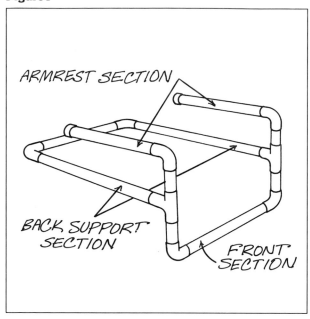

3. Assemble the back support section (**Figure E**).

4. The front section is identical to the back and front sections of the seat assembly (**Figure B**), but it is slightly longer. Substitute a G piece for the D piece shown in **Figure B**.

5. The completed arm assembly is shown in **Figure F**. Insert one end of the back section into the open J fitting in each armrest section, and install the front section at the bottom.

Final Frame Assembly

The assembled frame is shown in **Figure G**. An assistant will be most helpful during this stage of the game. The seat and arm assemblies are bolted together in three places on each side, as shown. Slip the arm assembly down over the seat assembly. The back section of the arm assembly should be about 1 inch above the holes that will house the rear sling rod, and it should extend about 2 inches beyond the back of the seat assembly. Tilt the front of the arm assembly upward as shown. Mark the positions for the bolt holes in both assemblies, and drill the holes. Reposition the two assemblies, insert the bolts from the outside in, and fasten each with a cap nut on the inside.

Making the Sling

The simple canvas sling has a casing at each end and is attached to the pipe frame by means of two rods, as shown in **Figure J**. It serves as a support for the cushion, and is removable for easy cleaning.

1. Cut one canvas Sling piece, 40 x 100 inches. Fold the piece in half lengthwise, placing right sides together, and stitch a 1-inch-wide seam along the long edge and one short edge, leaving the remaining short edge open and unstitched (**Figure H**). Clip the corners and turn the sling right side out.

2. Press the seam allowances to the inside along the short open edge and stitch the edges together.

3. Fold one short edge to the back of the sling, forming a 3¼-inch-wide casing (**Figure I**). Stitch the casing in place close to the edge as shown. Stitch again ¼ inch from the first stitching line. Make an identical casing at the opposite end of the sling, being careful to turn the edge to the same side of the sling.

Installing the Sling

The assembled chair, with the sling in place, is shown in **Figure J**.

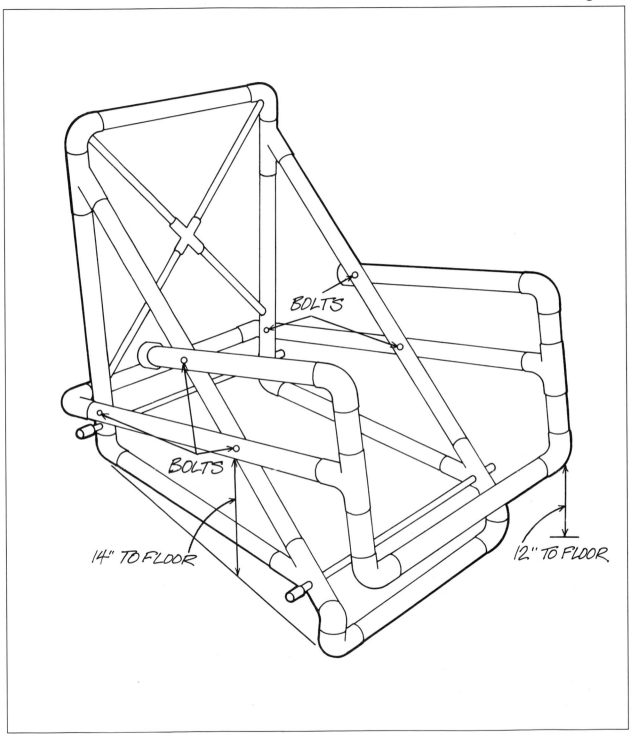

BOLTS

BOLTS

14" TO FLOOR

12." TO FLOOR

Figure H

Figure I

3¼"

Figure J

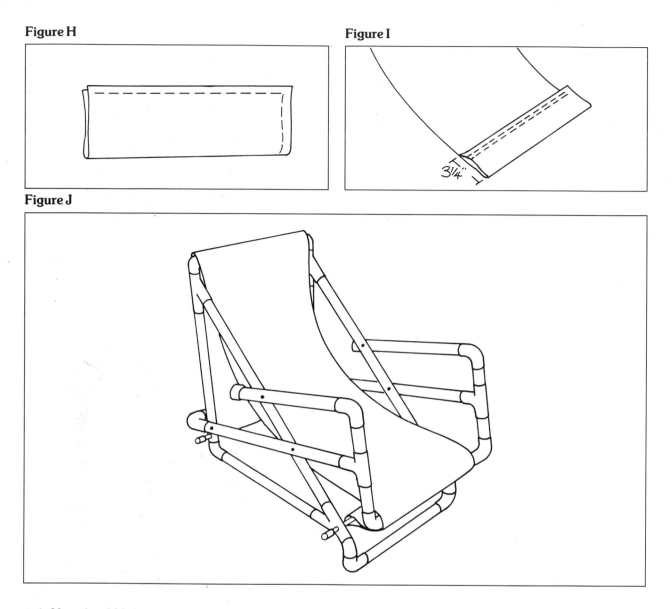

1. You should have two lengths of ¾-inch pipe left over from the frame assembly (the two **N** pieces). Insert one of these pieces through the holes in one side of the frame, near the front end (**Figure J**). Slide the pipe through the casing at one end of the sling, and continue to push it on through the holes in the opposite side of the frame. Leave equal extensions on each side of the frame, and install an end cap (**P** fitting) on each end of the pipe.

2. Insert the remaining pipe through the holes in one side of the frame near the back. Pull the upper end of the sling around the outside of the front crossbar on the arm assembly. Drape it over the top crossbar at the back of the frame, and pull it down to the bottom, inside the back crossbar of the arm assembly. Insert the pipe through the casing and push it on through the holes in the opposite side of the frame. Secure it with end caps. The sling should not be taut.

3. Place the chaise cushion on the sling and give it a test.

PVC Hammock

Put the lemonade in the refrigerator and by the time it's good and cold you can build this PVC hammock stand. Overall dimensions are 138 x 37 x 36 inches. The heavy cotton hammock takes only a few hours to stitch up. The structure is self-supporting so the only thing you need a tree for is the shade.

Figure A

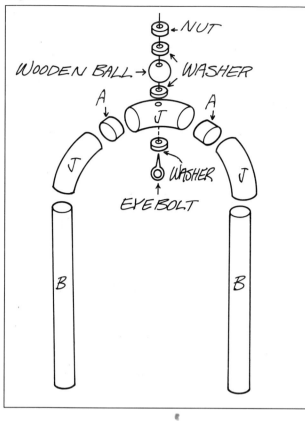

Materials

For the stand:

50 feet of straight 2½-inch PVC pipe

2½-inch PVC fittings: fourteen 45-degree angle joints; twelve Y-joints; four T-joints; and four end caps

PVC solvent cement or a handful of No. 6 gauge self-tapping sheet metal screws, each 1 inch long

Two 5-foot lengths of No. 8 chain

Six connecting links, each one size larger than the chain (You can eliminate the connecting links if you're strong enough to pry open the eye bolts to insert the chain.)

Four 4-inch-long eye bolts, each with two washers and a standard nut; and two 6-inch-long eye bolts, each with three washers and a standard nut

Two 1½-inch-diameter wooden macrame balls (A macrame ball is a sphere with a hole drilled through the center.)

For the hammock:

3½ yards of heavy cotton fabric (duck or canvas), 60 inches wide.

One standard-size bed pillow

Heavy-duty thread to match the fabric

Building the Stand

The hammock stand consists of six sections and six connecting bars. A yolk section (**Figure A**) is joined to two corner sections (**Figure B**) and a crossbar to form each end of the stand (**Figure C**). The two end assemblies are then joined by long connecting bars to form the complete stand (**Figure D**).

1. The required lengths of straight pipe listed below were calculated on the basis of ¾-inch fitting allowances. Check the depth of each fitting and, if necessary, recalculate the length of each straight piece of pipe to compensate for the difference on each end. Cut and label the straight pieces of pipe listed below. Label the fittings as listed.

Code	Length	Quantity
A	1⅜ inches	16
B	23 inches	4
C	9½ inches	4
D	9¼ inches	4
E	5 inches	4
F	26 inches	2
G	60 inches	2
H	68¼ inches	2
I	36 inches	2

Fittings:

J	45-degree joint
K	Y-joint
L	T-joint
M	End cap

2. Refer to **Figure A** as you assemble the pipe and fittings to form one yolk section. The short **A** pieces will be covered completely by the fittings they join.

3. The hammock will hang from an eye bolt inserted through the top of each yolk. On one yolk section, drill a hole straight down through the uppermost **J** fitting, in one side and out the other. Use a bit that is slightly larger in diameter than the 6-inch eye bolt shank. Place a washer on the eye bolt, insert the bolt through the hole from the bottom up, then install another washer, a wooden macrame ball, and a third washer. Fasten the assembly with a nut.

4. Make a second yolk section, repeating the procedures in steps 2 and 3.

5. Refer to **Figure B** as you assemble one corner section. Start with the bottom K fitting and assemble the parts in the order shown. The open end of the L fitting should face what will be the center of the hammock. Be sure the open end of the K fitting in the center of the upper arm is pointing in the direction shown. The top K fitting joins the two arms; slip it over the arm ends to complete the section.

6. Repeat the procedures in step 5 to assemble three more corner sections. When finished, the two corner sections for one side of the hammock should be mirror images of the two for the opposite side, with the open end of each L fitting facing the center of the stand.

7. Now assemble one complete end of the stand (**Figure C**). Insert a straight F piece into the open L fitting in one corner section. Add the second corner section and then install the assembled yolk section on top.

8. Repeat the procedures in step 7 to assemble the opposite end of the stand.

9. Don't break out the lemonade just yet, but make sure it's getting cold. Connect the two assembled ends, using a G and an H piece at each side (**Figure D**).

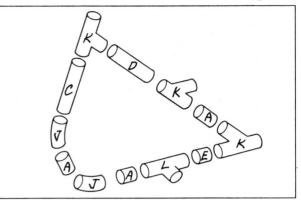

Figure B

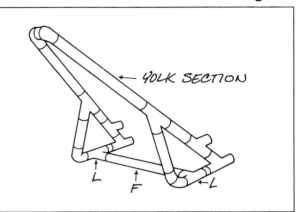

Figure C

← YOLK SECTION

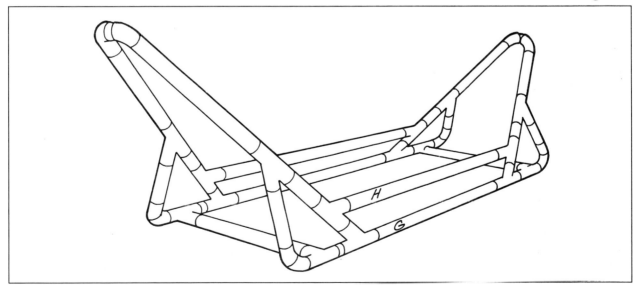

Figure D

Figure E

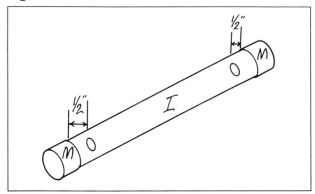

10. The I pieces will support the ends of the fabric hammock. Install an end cap (**M**) on each end of one I piece. Drill a hole straight down through the pipe, in one side and out the other, placing the center of the hole ½ inch from the end cap (**Figure E**). Use a bit that is slightly larger in diameter than the 4-inch eye bolt shank. Slip a washer onto the eye bolt, insert the bolt through the hole, add another washer, and secure it

with a nut. Drill a hole through the pipe near the opposite end in the same manner, making sure that it is drilled along the same axis as the first hole. Install an eye bolt, with washers and nut.

11. Repeat the procedures in step 10 using the remaining I piece, M fittings, and eye bolts.

Making the Hammock

The fabric hammock is a large, double-layered rectangle with a casing at each end to accommodate the pipe support. We made a simple organizer that is sewn into one of the side seams. It hangs from the hammock, and will hold magazines, eyeglasses, writing paper, and other necessities of lazy living. The pillow is covered in the same fabric, but is not attached to the hammock.

1. All of the required fabric pieces are listed below. A cutting diagram is provided in **Figure F**.

        Hammock, 30 x 87 inches – cut two
        Organizer, 15 x 16½ inches – cut two
        Pocket, 10½ x 15 inches – cut one
        Pillow, 20 x 30 inches – cut two

Figure F

HAMMOCK 30" x 87"	PILLOW 20" x 30"	POCKET 10½" x 15"
		ORGANIZER 15" x 16½"
HAMMOCK 30" x 87"	PILLOW 20" x 30"	ORGANIZER 15" x 16½"

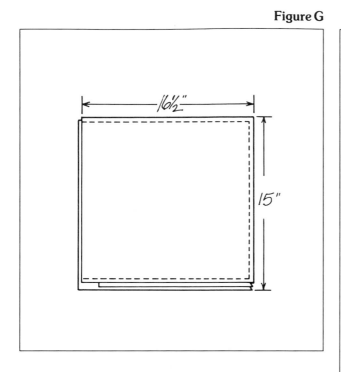

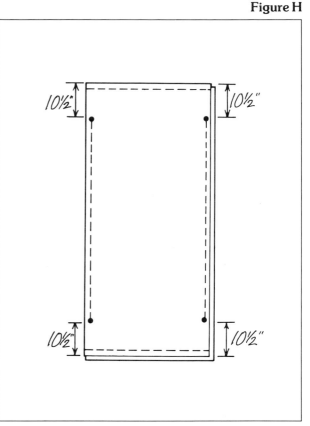

2. Stitch up the organizer first, so it can be sewn into a side seam of the hammock body. On the Pocket piece, press a ½-inch-wide hem to the wrong side of the fabric along one long edge only. Stitch the hem.

3. Place one Organizer piece right side up on a flat surface. Place the Pocket piece on top, right side up, aligning the unhemmed long edge of the Pocket piece with one 15-inch edge of the Organizer piece. Place the remaining Organizer piece on top, right side down, and pin the layers together along each edge. Stitch a ½-inch-wide seam along the three edges that include the Pocket piece, leaving the remaining edge open and unstitched (**Figure G**).

4. Clip the corners, turn the stitched organizer right side out, and press. Baste the open edges together, ¼ inch from the raw edges.

5. Place one Hammock piece right side up on a flat surface. Place the organizer on top, aligning the basted edge with one side edge of the Hammock piece. You can place the organizer equally distant from each end, or closer to one end than the other for easy reaching. Place the remaining Hammock piece on top, right side down, and pin the layers together along each edge.

6. Stitch a ½-inch-wide seam along each short edge. Stitch a ½-inch-wide seam along each long edge, leaving 10½ inches open and unstitched at each end as shown in **Figure H**. The openings will form the casings for the pipe supports. Press the seams open.

7. Turn the hammock right side out. Press the seam allowances to the inside along the open portions of each side seam. Stitch these allowances in place.

8. To make the pillow cover, pin the two Pillow pieces right sides together. Stitch a ½-inch-wide seam along each long edge and one short edge, leaving the remaining short edge open. Clip the corners and press the seams open.

9. Turn the stitched pillow cover right side out and press the seam allowances to the inside along the open edges. Insert the pillow and stitch the open edges together. (To make a removable cover, simply hem the open edges.)

Figure I

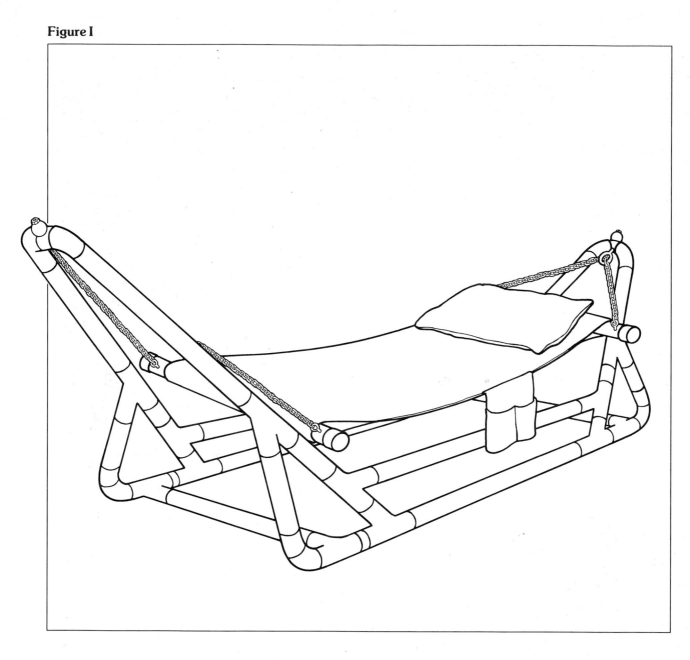

Final Assembly

1. Find the I pieces with end caps and eye bolts that you assembled in steps 10 and 11 of "Building the Stand." Insert one of these through the casing at one end of the fabric hammock. Insert the other through the casing at the opposite end.

2. The hammock is attached to the stand with a 5-foot length of chain at each end (**Figure I**). Use a connecting link to attach each end of each chain to an eye bolt, as shown. Use an additional connecting link to attach the center link of each chain to the eye bolt at one end of the hammock stand.

3. Find some shade and pour the lemonade.

Patio Chair

This chair is a lazy person's dream – it's tremendously easy to build, it has an adjustable back that helps make it a real delight to sit in, and you don't have to make a special cushion because it's designed to take a standard patio chair cushion. What more could you want? Overall dimensions of the redwood frame are 28 x 41 x 33 inches.

Figure A

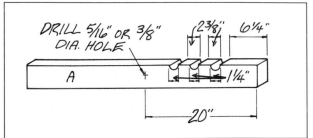

DRILL 5/16" OR 3/8" DIA. HOLE

A

2 3/8" 6 1/4"

1 1/4"

20"

Figure B

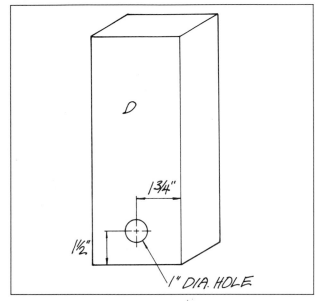

D

1 3/4"

1 1/2"

1" DIA. HOLE

Materials

Redwood: We used the six different sizes of standard dimensional redwood listed below, which require only cross cuts and no rip cuts to produce the chair parts. If you don't mind making the extra rip cuts, you may prefer to recalculate and purchase only two different sizes from which to cut the parts, as you may save a little money by doing so. We used:

6 linear feet of 2 x 2 redwood
3 linear feet of 2 x 3 redwood
25 linear feet of 2 x 4 redwood
4 linear feet of 2 x 6 redwood
2 linear feet of 2 x 8 redwood
7 linear feet of 1 x 2 redwood
4-foot length of 1-inch wooden dowel rod

Flathead wood screws: forty-four No. 12 gauge, each 2½ inches long; ten No. 6 gauge, each 1½ inches long; and two No. 6 gauge, each ¾ inches long

Four ¼ x 3½ roundhead carriage bolts, each with one flat washer and a nut

Two flat metal washers, each 2 inches in diameter with a 1⅛-inch center hole

One standard patio chair cushion, 19 to 23 inches wide, 40 to 46 inches long, and as thick as you like

The patio chair consists of three basic assemblies: a long rectangular seat frame that includes the front and back legs with an axle and wheels, a shorter rectangular back frame with a support structure that allows it to be adjusted, and two identical armrest assemblies.

Cutting the Parts

1. Cut the parts listed below from the specified materials and label each part with its identifying code.

Code	Length	Quantity	Material
A	41 inches	2	2 x 4
B	16 inches	3	2 x 4
C	12 inches	2	2 x 4
D	10½ inches	2	2 x 4
E	12¼ inches	2	1 x 2
F	16 inches	3	1 x 2
G	11½ inches	4	2 x 4
H	18 inches	2	2 x 6
I	24 inches	2	2 x 4
J	16 inches	4	2 x 2
K	11½ inches	2	2 x 3

2. The A pieces will serve as the side members of the seat frame and must be notched to provide various angles of support for the seat back assembly. (If that sounds confusing, it might help to see what these assemblies look like. The assembled seat frame is shown in **Figure J** and the entire assembled chair is shown in **Figure M**.) A cutting diagram for the A pieces is provided in **Figure A**. Refer to this diagram as you cut or drill three rounded notches across one long edge of one A piece. Drill a ⁵⁄₁₆- or ⅜-inch-diameter hole through the board where indicated on the drawing, to accommodate the bolt that joins the seat and back frames. Use this A piece as a guide to modify the second A piece,

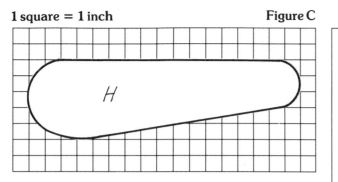

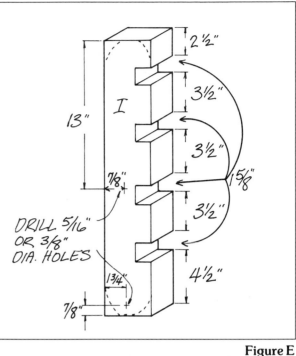

so the notches and holes will be perfectly aligned.

3. The D pieces will serve as the back legs and must be drilled to accommodate the axle. Drill a 1-inch-diameter hole through one D piece, placing the center of the hole midway between the long edges and 1½ inches from one short end as shown in **Figure B**. This will be the lower end of the leg. Use the drilled D piece as a guide to drill the second D piece so the holes will be aligned properly.

4. The H pieces will serve as the armrests. A scale drawing for the contoured armrest is provided in **Figure C**. Enlarge the drawing and cut the contours on the two H pieces.

5. The I pieces will serve as the side members of the back frame and must be dadoed to accommodate the back slats. A cutting diagram is provided in **Figure D**. Refer to the diagram as you cut four dadoes across one long edge of one I piece, making each dado 1½ inches wide and 1½ inches deep. Space the dadoes as shown. In addition, drill two ⁵⁄₁₆- or ³⁄₈-inch-diameter holes through the board where indicated on the diagram, to accommodate the bolts that join the back frame to the back support assembly and to the seat frame. Finally, round off both ends of the board as shown. Use the modified I piece as a guide to cut and drill the second I piece.

6. The K pieces will serve as back supports. They must be drilled to accommodate a dowel cross brace and the bolts that join the back supports to the back frame. A cutting diagram is provided in **Figure E**. Drill the holes in one K support where indicated and then round off both ends of the board as shown. Use the modified K piece as a guide to cut and drill the second K piece.

Figure E

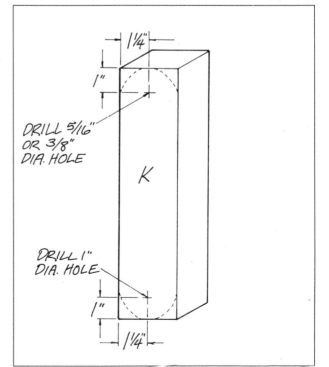

Figure F

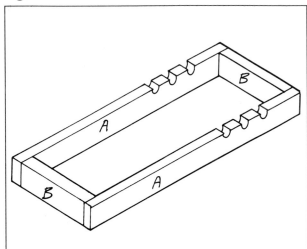

Figure G

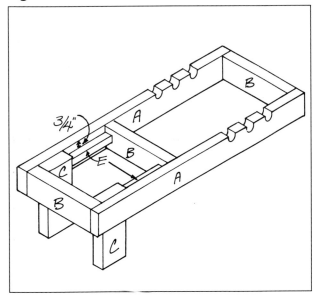

7. Cut two wheels from the redwood 2 x 8, making each a 6-inch-diameter circle. Drill a 1⅛-inch-diameter hole through the exact center of each wheel.

8. We cut thin circular covers for the axle ends, for a more finished look. If you wish to do this you'll need to slice some of the scrap stock down to a thickness of about ⅛ inch, give or take a little. You'll need enough of the thin stock to cut two circular pieces, each 2¼ inches in diameter. Label each piece L.

Building the Seat Frame

1. To begin, assemble a simple rectangle using two of the B pieces and both of the A pieces as shown in **Figure F**. The B pieces should be placed between the A pieces, flush with the ends. Be sure that the A pieces are turned the same way end for end, that the notched edge of each A piece faces the same direction, and that the A pieces cover the ends of the B pieces. For reference, the notched side of the frame will be the top, and the B piece farthest from the notches will be the front of the frame. Secure each glued joint using two of the longest screws.

2. Add the third B piece as a cross-frame member between the A pieces, 16 inches from the front B piece. Secure each end using two of the longest screws.

3. The C pieces will serve as the front legs. Place one leg C inside one front corner of the seat frame so that the top of the leg is flush with the upper edges of the frame pieces. The leg should be turned so that one edge is butted against the front B frame member and one wide side is butted against the side A frame member. Secure the leg with glue and two of the longest screws. Attach the remaining front leg C in the opposite front corner of the frame.

4. The E pieces will serve as support strips for the seat slats. Glue one E piece to the inside of one side frame member A, between the front leg and the center B frame member. The upper edge of the support strip E should be ¾ inch from the upper edge of the A member as shown in **Figure G**. Secure the support strip using two of the 1½-inch screws. Attach the remaining support strip E to the inside of the A member on the opposite side of the frame.

5. The three F pieces will serve as the seat slats. Place them flat across the frame with the ends resting on the support strips E. Butt the front slat against the front legs and allow about 3 inches of space between slats. The third slat will be about 1¾ inches from the center B frame member. Be sure that the slats are turned so that each is resting on a wide side and does not extend up past the upper edges of the frame. Secure each end of each slat by inserting one of the 1½-inch screws down through the slat into the support strip.

6. At the back of the frame, install a back leg D in

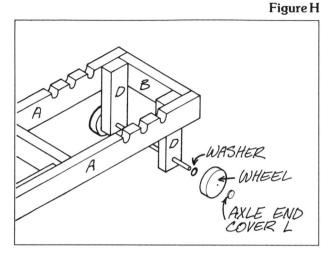

Figure I

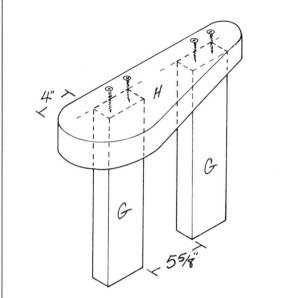

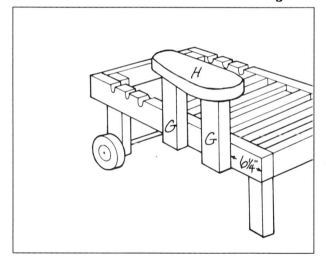

each corner as you did the front legs. Be sure that the drilled end of each leg is at the bottom.

7. Cut a 20-inch length of dowel rod to serve as the axle. Insert the axle through the aligned holes in the back legs, leaving equal extensions on each side, and glue the axle in place.

8. The wheel installation is illustrated in **Figure H**. Lubricate the center hole of each wheel using beeswax or hard soap. At each end of the axle install a metal washer and a wheel. The axle should extend beyond the wheel, to allow enough space for the wheel to turn easily. Glue a circular cover L over the end of the axle and secure it using one of the short screws.

Adding the Arm Assemblies

1. Each arm assembly consists of an armrest H and two supports G, assembled as shown in **Figure I**. The supports should be flush with the straight edge of the armrest, and there should be 5⅝ inches of space between the supports. The front support should be about 4 inches from the front end of the armrest. Glue together one arm assembly and secure the joints by inserting two of the long screws down through the armrest into each support.

2. Build a second arm assembly in the same manner, using the remaining armrest H and supports G. Be sure the arm assemblies are mirror images of each other.

3. Glue one arm assembly to the outside of the seat frame, against one of the A members, placing the front

G support 6¼ inches from the front of the frame as shown in **Figure J**. The lower ends of the supports should be flush with the lower edge of the A frame member. Note that the straight edge of the armrest faces the center of the frame. Secure the joints by inserting two long screws through each support into the A member. Attach the remaining arm assembly to the opposite side of the frame in the same manner.

Figure L

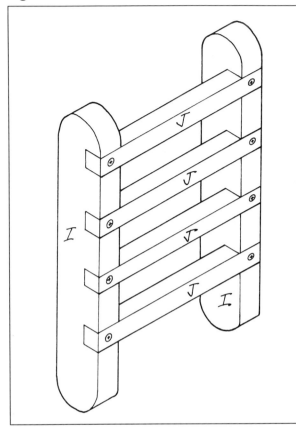

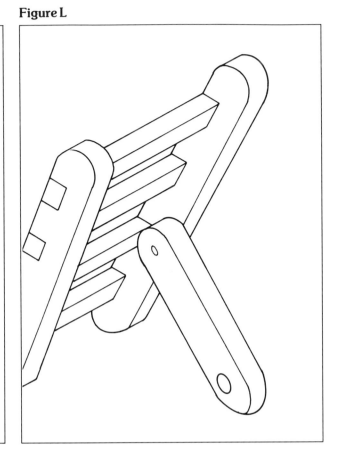

Building the Back Assemblies

1. The back frame consists of two side members I and four slats J. Place the two side members on their uncut long edges, about 16 inches apart, and glue the four slats into the aligned dadoes as shown in **Figure K**. Secure the joints by inserting a long screw through each end of each slat into the side member.

2. Place one of the back supports K against the inside of one side frame member I, aligning the bolt holes as shown in **Figure L**. Insert a bolt from the outside of the frame member through both pieces, and secure it with a washer and nut. Don't tighten the nut too much, as the back supports should be able to swivel fairly easily. Attach the remaining back support K to the inside of the opposite frame member I.

3. Cut a 19-inch length of dowel to serve as the lower back support. Insert it through the large holes at the free ends of the back supports K, leaving equal extensions on each side.

Final Assembly

The completely assembled chair frame is shown in **Figure M**. To attach the back assemblies to the seat frame, slide the lower drilled ends of the back frame members I down inside the seat frame, just behind the center B member, and adjust them to align the bolt holes in the I pieces with those in the A pieces. On each side, insert a bolt from the outside through both pieces, and secure it loosely on the inside with a washer and nut. Pivot the back support assembly downward and slide the dowel rod ends into a set of aligned notches in the A frame members. Add the cushion and you're ready for mint juleps on the verandah.

PATIO CHAIR

Chaise Lounge

The chaise is a slightly longer twin of the patio chair, being equally easy to build and enjoy. It's designed to take a standard chaise lounge patio cushion. The length and width of either of these pieces are easily altered to accommodate exceptionally large or small loungers. Overall dimensions of the frame are 28 x 68 x 33 inches.

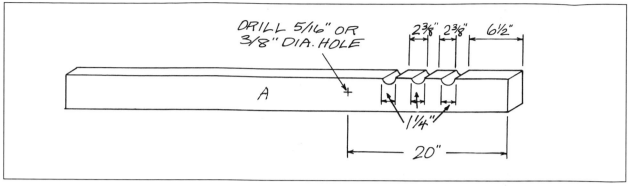

Materials

Redwood: We used the six different sizes of standard dimensional redwood listed below, which require only cross cuts and no rip cuts to produce the parts. If you don't mind making the extra rip cuts, you may prefer to recalculate and purchase only two different sizes from which to cut the parts, as you may save a little money by doing so. We used:

6 linear feet of 2 x 2 redwood
3 linear feet of 2 x 3 redwood
30 linear feet of 2 x 4 redwood
4 linear feet of 2 x 6 redwood
2 linear feet of 2 x 8 redwood
20 linear feet of 1 x 2 redwood

4-foot length of 1-inch wooden dowel rod

Flathead wood screws: forty-four No. 12 gauge, each 2½ inches long; twenty-six No. 6 gauge, each 1½ inches long; and two No. 6 gauge, each ¾ inches long

Four ¼ x 3½ roundhead carriage bolts, each with one flat washer and a nut

Two flat metal washers, each 2 inches in diameter with a 1⅛-inch center hole

One standard chaise lounge cushion, 19 to 23 inches wide, 65 to 72 inches long, and as thick as you like

These instructions are going to be a bit of deja vu if you have already built the patio chair. The chaise lounge consists of three basic assemblies: a long rectangular seat frame that includes the front and back legs with an axle and wheels, a shorter rectangular back frame with a support structure that allows it to be adjusted, and two identical armrest assemblies.

Cutting the Parts

1. Cut the parts listed below from the specified materials and label each part with its identifying code.

Code	Length	Quantity	Material
A	68 inches	2	2 x 4
B	16 inches	3	2 x 4
C	12 inches	2	2 x 4
D	10½ inches	2	2 x 4
E	39⅜ inches	2	1 x 2
F	16 inches	9	1 x 2
G	11½ inches	4	2 x 4
H	18 inches	2	2 x 6
I	24 inches	2	2 x 4
J	16 inches	4	2 x 2
K	11½ inches	2	2 x 3

2. The A pieces will serve as the side members of the seat frame and must be notched to provide various angles of support for the seat back assembly. (If that sounds confusing, it might help to see what these assemblies look like. The assembled seat frame is shown in **Figure J** and the entire assembled chaise is shown in **Figure M**.) A cutting diagram for the A pieces is provided in **Figure A**. Refer to this diagram as you cut or drill three rounded notches across one long edge of one A piece. Drill a ⁵⁄₁₆- or ⅜-inch-diameter hole through the board where indicated on the drawing, to accommodate the bolt that joins the seat and back frames. Use this A piece as a guide to modify the second A piece, so the notches and holes will be perfectly aligned.

Figure B

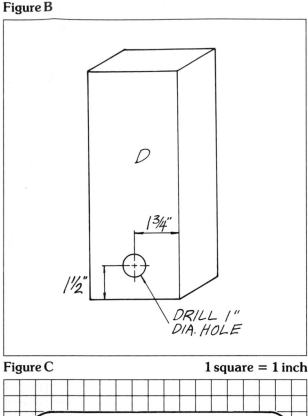

Figure C   1 square = 1 inch

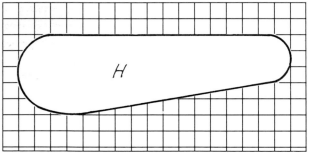

Figure D

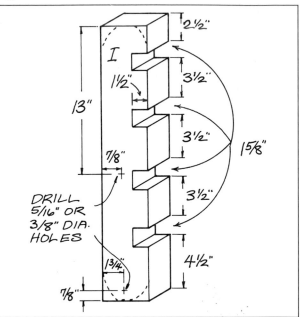

3. The D pieces will serve as the back legs and must be drilled to accommodate the axle. Drill a 1-inch-diameter hole through one D piece, placing the center of the hole midway between the long edges and 1½ inches from one short end as shown in **Figure B**. This will be the lower end of the leg. Use the drilled D piece as a guide to drill the second D piece so the holes will be aligned properly.

4. The H pieces will serve as the armrests. A scale drawing for the contoured armrest is provided in **Figure C**. Enlarge the drawing and cut the contours on the two H pieces.

5. The I pieces will serve as the side members of the back frame and must be dadoed to accommodate the back slats. A cutting diagram is provided in **Figure D**. Refer to the diagram as you cut four dadoes across one long edge of one I piece, making each dado 1½ inches wide and 1½ inches deep. Space the dadoes as shown. In addition, drill two 5/16- or 3/8-inch-diameter holes through the board where indicated on the diagram, to accommodate the bolts that join the back frame to the back support assembly and to the seat frame. Finally, round off both ends of the boards as shown. Use the modified I piece as a guide to cut and drill the second I piece.

6. The K pieces will serve as back supports. They must be drilled to accommodate a dowel cross brace and the bolts that join the back supports to the back frame. A cutting diagram is provided in **Figure E**. Drill the holes in one K support where indicated and then round off both ends of the board as shown. Use the modified K piece as a guide to cut and drill the second K piece.

7. Cut two wheels from the redwood 2 x 8, making each a 6-inch-diameter circle. Drill a 1⅛-inch-diameter hole through the exact center of each wheel.

8. We cut thin circular covers for the axle ends, for a more finished look. If you wish to do this you'll need to slice some of the scrap stock down to a thickness of about ⅛ inch, give or take a little. You'll need enough of the thin stock to cut two circular pieces, each 2¼ inches in diameter. Label each piece L.

Building the Seat Frame

1. To begin, assemble a simple rectangle using two of the B pieces and both of the A pieces as shown in **Figure F**. The B pieces should be placed between the A pieces, flush with the ends. Be sure that the A pieces are turned the same way end for end, that the notched edge of each A piece faces the same direction, and that the A pieces cover the ends of the B pieces. For reference, the notched side of the frame will be the top, and the B piece farthest from the notches will be the front of the frame. Secure each glued joint using two of the longest screws.

2. Add the third B piece as a cross-frame member between the A pieces, 44½ inches from the front B piece. Secure each end using two of the longest screws.

3. The C pieces will serve as the front legs. Place one leg C inside one front corner of the seat frame so that the top of the leg is flush with the upper edges of the frame pieces. The leg should be turned so that one edge is butted against the front B frame member and

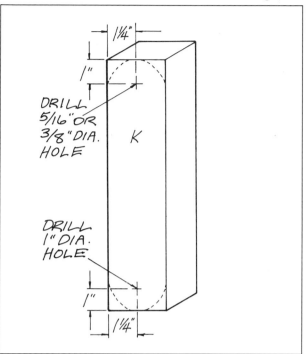

one wide side is butted against the side A frame member. Secure the leg with glue and two of the longest screws. Attach the remaining front leg C in the opposite front corner of the frame.

Figure F

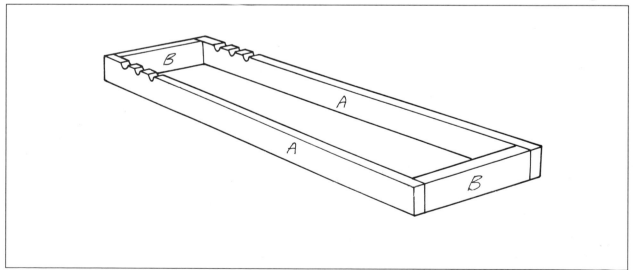

Figure G

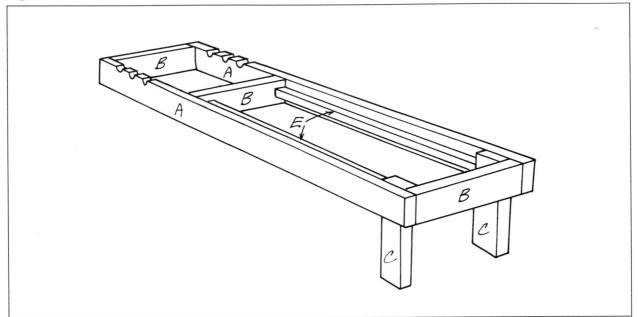

Figure H

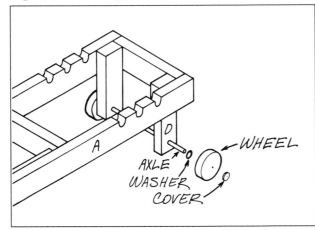

4. The E pieces will serve as support strips for the seat slats. Glue one E piece to the inside of one side frame member A, between the front leg and the center B frame member. The upper edge of the support strip E should be ¾ inch from the upper edge of the A member as shown in **Figure G**. Secure the support strip using four of the 1½-inch screws. Attach the remaining support strip E to the inside of the A member on the opposite side of the frame.

5. The nine F pieces will serve as the seat slats. Place them flat across the frame with the ends resting on the support strips E. Butt the front slat against the front legs and allow about 3 inches of space between slats. The last slat will be about 1¼ inches from the center B frame member. Be sure that the slats are turned so that each is resting on a wide side and does not extend up past the upper edges of the frame. Secure each end of each slat by inserting one of the 1½-inch screws down through the slat into the support strip.

6. At the back of the frame, install a back leg D in each corner as you did the front legs. Be sure that the drilled end of each leg is at the bottom.

7. Cut a 20-inch length of dowel rod to serve as the axle. Insert the axle through the aligned holes in the back legs, leaving equal extensions on each side, and glue the axle in place.

8. The wheel installation is illustrated in **Figure H**. Lubricate the center hole of each wheel using beeswax or hard soap. At each end of the axle install a metal washer and a wheel. The axle should extend beyond the wheel, to allow enough space for the wheel to turn easily. Glue a circular cover L over the end of the axle and secure it using one of the short screws.

Figure I

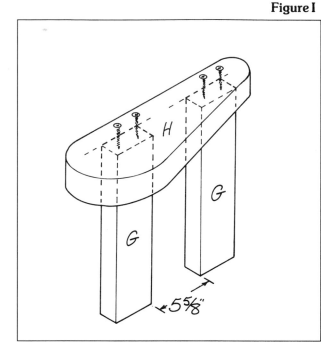

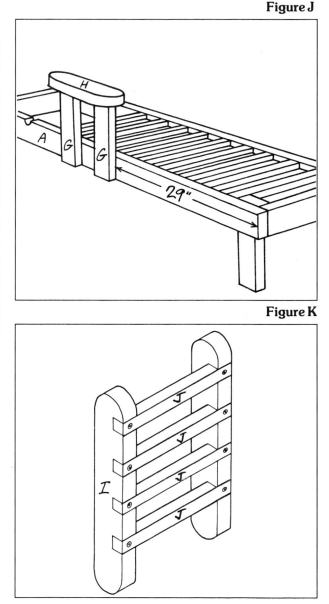

Adding the Arm Assemblies

1. Each arm assembly consists of an armrest H and two supports G, assembled as shown in **Figure I**. The supports should be flush with the straight edge of the armrest, and there should be 5⅝ inches of space between the supports. The front support should be about 4 inches from the front end of the armrest. Glue together one arm assembly and secure the joints by inserting two of the long screws down through the armrest into each support.

2. Build a second arm assembly in the same manner, using the remaining armrest H and supports G. Be sure the arm assemblies are mirror images of each other.

3. Glue one arm assembly to the outside of the seat frame, against one of the A members, placing the front G support 29 inches from the front of the frame as shown in **Figure J**. The lower ends of the supports should be flush with the lower edge of the A frame member. Note that the straight edge of the armrest faces the center of the frame. Secure the joints by inserting two long screws through each support into the A member. Attach the remaining arm assembly to the opposite side of the frame in the same manner.

Building the Back Assemblies

1. The back frame consists of two side members I and four slats J. Place the two side members on their uncut long edges, about 16 inches apart, and glue the four slats into the aligned dadoes as shown in **Figure K**. Secure the joints by inserting a long screw through each end of each slat into the side member.

Figure L

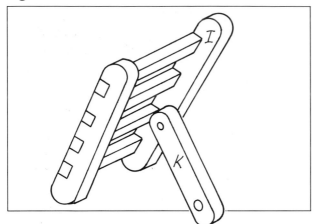

2. Place one of the back supports **K** against the inside of one side frame member **I**, aligning the bolt holes as shown in **Figure L**. Insert a bolt from the outside of the frame member through both pieces, and secure it with a washer and nut. Don't tighten the nut too much, as the back supports should be able to swivel fairly easily.

Attach the remaining support **K** to the opposite frame member **I**.

3. Cut a 19-inch length of dowel for the lower support. Insert it through the holes at the ends of the back supports, with equal extensions on each side.

Final Assembly

The assembled chair frame is shown in **Figure M**. To attach the back assemblies to the seat frame, slide the lower drilled ends of the back frame members **I** down inside the seat frame, just behind the center **B** member, and align the bolt holes in the **I** pieces with those in the **A** pieces. On each side, insert a bolt from the outside through both pieces, and secure it loosely with a washer and nut. Pivot the back support downward and slide the dowel rod ends into a set of notches in the **A** frame members. Add the cushion. If you made the patio chair and have already had mint juleps on the verandah, the chaise calls for something a little longer and taller — perhaps a Long Island tea by the hot tub.

Figure M

Patio Rocker

We've had lots of requests for a patio rocking chair, so here it is, folks. It has turned out to be our most sought-after patio furnishing by both young and young-at-heart alike. You'll find that it's very similar in construction to the patio chair and chaise, and takes a standard patio chair cushion. Overall dimensions are 28 x 40 x 36 inches

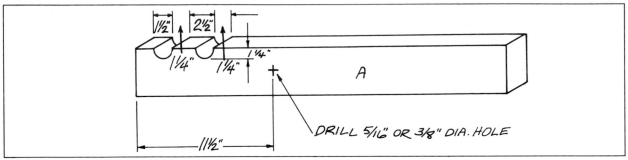

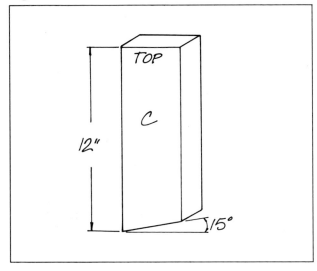

(**Note:** Purchase two 8-foot-long boards to make up the required amount of redwood 1 x 8.)

2-foot length of 1-inch wooden dowel rod

Four ¼ x 3½ roundhead carriage bolts, each with a flat washer and nut

Twenty-four 4d finishing nails

Flathead wood screws: fifty-two No. 12 gauge, each 2½ inches long; and twenty-two No. 6 gauge, each 1½ inches long

One standard patio chair cushion, 19 to 23 inches wide, 40 to 46 inches long, and as thick as you like

The patio rocker consists of four basic types of assemblies: a long rectangular seat frame that is similar to the seat frames of the patio chair and chaise, a shorter rectangular back section with a support structure that allows it to be adjusted, two identical armrest assemblies, and two identical rocker-and-leg assemblies.

Materials

Redwood: We used the seven different sizes of standard dimensional redwood listed below, which require primarily only cross cuts and very few rip cuts to produce the chair parts. If you don't mind making the extra rip cuts, you may prefer to recalculate and purchase only two different sizes from which to cut the parts, as you may save some money that way. We used:

6 linear feet of redwood 2 x 2
3 linear feet of redwood 2 x 3
24 linear feet of redwood 2 x 4
4 linear feet of redwood 2 x 6
8 linear feet of redwood 2 x 8
10 linear feet of redwood 1 x 2
16 linear feet of redwood 1 x 8

Cutting the Parts

1. Cut the parts listed below from 2 x 4 redwood and label each part with its identifying code.

Code	Length	Quantity
A	32½ inches	2
B	16 inches	3
C	12 inches	2
D	14¼ inches	2
E	24 inches	2
F	11½ inches	4

2. The A pieces will serve as the side members of the seat frame and must be notched to provide two different angles of support for the seat back assembly. (See

Figure C

Figure H, which shows the assembled seat frame, and Figure O, which shows the entire assembled chair, if you want some enlightenment here.) A cutting diagram for the A pieces is provided in Figure A. Refer to this diagram as you cut or drill two rounded notches across one long edge of one A piece. In addition, drill a 5/16- or 3/8-inch-diameter hole through the board where indicated on the drawing, to accommodate the bolt that joins the seat and back frames. Use this A piece as a guide to modify the second A piece, so the notches and holes will be perfectly aligned.

3. The C pieces will serve as the back legs. The lower end of each back leg must be mitered so that it will fit squarely on top of the rocker. Miter one end of each C piece at a 15-degree angle as shown in Figure B, cutting carefully so you do not shorten the board on the long side of the miter cut.

4. The D pieces will serve as the front legs and must also be mitered to fit on top of the rockers. Miter one end of each D piece as you did the C pieces, but cut the D pieces at a a 10-degree angle instead of a 15-degree angle.

5. The E pieces will serve as the side members of the back section and must be dadoed to accommodate the back slats. A cutting diagram is provided in Figure C. Refer to the diagram as you cut four dadoes across one long edge of one E piece, making each dado 1½ inches wide and 1½ inches deep. Space the dadoes as shown. In addition, drill two 5/16- or 3/8-inch-diameter holes through the board where indicated on the diagram, to accommodate the bolts that join the back section to the back supports and to the seat frame. Finally, round off both ends of the board as shown. Use the modified E piece as a guide to cut and drill the second E piece, so the dadoes and holes will be aligned properly.

6. Cut the parts listed below from redwood 1 x 2 and label each part with its identifying code.

Code	Length	Quantity
G	4½ inches	2
H	7½ inches	2
I	3½ inches	2
J	16 inches	3
K	13 inches	2

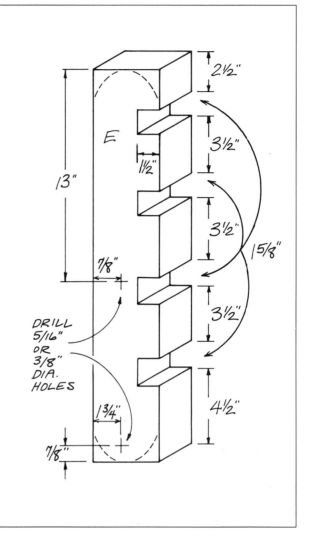

7. Cut the parts listed below from the designated materials and label each with its identifying code.

Code	Length	Quantity	Material
L	40 inches	2	2 x 8
M	40 inches	4	1 x 8
N	16 inches	4	2 x 2
O	11 inches	2	2 x 3
P	18 inches	2	2 x 6
Q	19 inches	1	dowel

Figure D   1 square = 1 inch

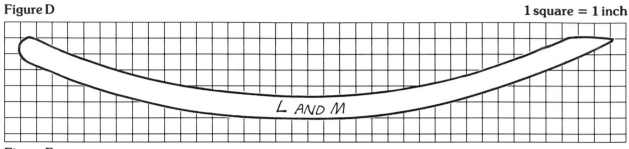

L AND M

Figure E

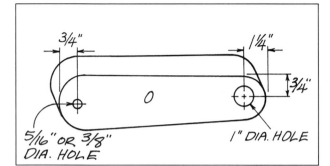

3/4"   1¼"

O

3/4"

5/16" OR 3/8"
DIA. HOLE   1" DIA. HOLE

Figure F   1 square = 1 inch

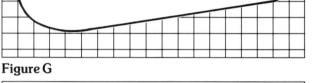

P

Figure G

8. Each rocker is 3 inches thick, the thickness being achieved by glueing together a rocker sandwich, if you will. The two thin bread layers are cut from **M** pieces, and the thick baloney layer is cut from an **L** piece. A scale drawing for the rocker is provided in **Figure D**. Enlarge the drawing to make a full-size pattern, and contour each of the **L** and **M** pieces.

9. The **O** pieces will serve as the back supports. Each must be drilled to accommodate a dowel cross-support and a bolt that joins the back support to the back section. A cutting diagram is provided in **Figure E**. Drill the holes through one **O** piece where indicated. Evenly taper and round off the upper end as shown. Round off and taper the lower end, cutting it quite close to the large hole on one side. Use this **O** piece as a guide to cut and drill the second **O** piece.

10. The **P** pieces will serve as the armrests. A scale drawing for the contoured armrest is provided in **Figure F**. Enlarge the drawing and cut the contours on both **P** pieces. (**Note:** If you built the patio chair or chaise, the pattern that you made for the armrest is the same as this one.)

Building the Seat Section

1. Assemble a simple rectangle using the two **A** pieces and two of the **B** pieces, butting the ends as shown in **Figure G**. Place the **B** pieces between the **A** pieces, flush with the ends. Be sure that the **A** pieces are turned the same way end for end, that the notched edge of each **A** piece faces the same direction, and that the **A** pieces cover the ends of the **B** pieces. For reference, the notched side of the frame will be the top and the **B** piece farthest from the notches will be the front of the frame. Secure each glued joint using two of the long screws.

BUILDING OUTDOOR FURNITURE

2. Add the third B piece between the A pieces, 13½ inches from the back end of the frame (**Figure H**). Secure each end using two long screws.

3. The G, H, and I pieces serve as support strips for the seat slats. **Figure H** shows placement of the G and H support strips. Glue one G piece to the inside of one side frame member A, butting the front end of the support strip against the front frame member B. The upper edge of the support strip should be ¾ inch below the upper edge of the A member, and the strip should be rotated so that a wide side, not an edge, is against the A member as shown. Glue one H piece to the inside of the same A frame member, butting the back end of the strip against the middle frame member B as shown. This strip also should be placed ¾ inch below the upper edge of the A frame member, and rotated in the same manner. Glue the remaining G and H support strips to the inside of the A frame member on the opposite side of the frame, and secure each strip by inserting two of the shorter screws through the strip into the frame member A. The I support strips and the seat slats will be added later.

Building the Leg Sections

1. Refer to **Figure I** as you build one rocker-and-leg section. To make a rocker sandwich, simply glue one thick contoured rocker L between two thin rockers M. Clamp the assembly until the glue dries. Secure it by driving six finishing nails into each side of the rocker.

2. Glue a back leg C to the middle layer of the rocker, placing the mitered end of the leg at the bottom and the longer edge toward the front, so it sits flat on the rocker. The leg should be approximately 12½ inches from the back end of the rocker, measuring along the top of the rocker as shown in **Figure I**. Secure the leg by inserting two of the longer screws up through the rocker into the end of the leg.

3. Glue a front leg D to the rocker in the same manner, turning it so the longer edge is toward the back and allowing approximately 6½ inches from the rounded front end of the rocker to the leg. The horizontal distance between the front and back legs should be 14 inches. Secure the front leg using two screws as you did

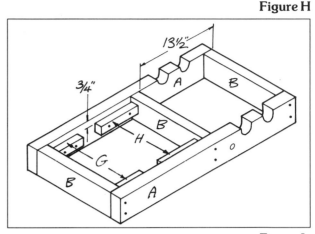

Figure I

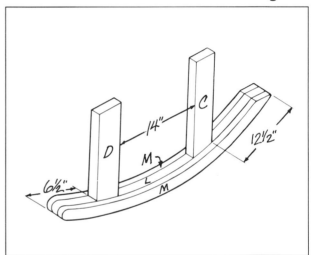

the back leg.

4. Build a second identical rocker-and-leg assembly in the same manner.

Building the Back Section

1. The back section, shown in **Figure J**, consists of two side members E and four slats N. Place the two side members on their uncut long edges, about 16 inches apart, making sure they are turned the same way end for end. Place the four slats across the side members, inserting the ends into the dadoes and adjusting so that the ends of the slats are flush with the outer edges of the side members as shown. Glue the slats into the

Figure J

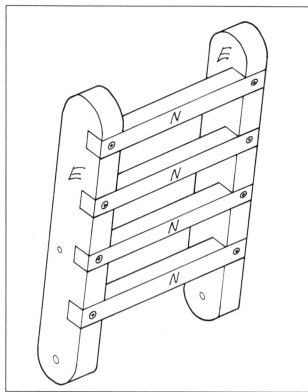

Figure K

dadoes and secure the joints by inserting a long screw through each end of each slat into the side member.

2. Place one of the back supports O against the inside of one side member E, aligning the bolt holes as shown in **Figure K**. The support should be rotated so that the larger hole at the lower end is closest to the edge facing us in the drawing. Insert a bolt from the outside of the E member through both pieces, and secure it on the inside with a washer and nut. Don't tighten the nut too much, as the back supports should be able to swivel fairly easily. Attach the remaining back support O to the inside of the other E piece in the same manner.

3. Insert the Q dowel through the larger holes at the lower ends of the O pieces, leaving equal extensions on each side. Glue the dowel in place in the holes.

Building the Arm Sections

1. Each arm assembly consists of an armrest P and two supports F. They are assembled as shown in **Fig-**

ure L. The supports should be flush with the straight edge of the armrest, and there should be about 5½ inches of space between the supports. The front support should be about 4 inches from the front end of the armrest. Glue together one arm assembly and secure the joints by inserting two of the long screws down through the armrest into each support.

2. Build a second arm assembly in the same manner, using the remaining armrest P and supports F. The two arm assemblies should be mirror images of each other.

Assembly

1. The lower chair assembly is shown in **Figure M**. Begin by placing the two rocker-and-leg assemblies about 14 inches apart, making certain they are both turned the same way end for end. Lower the seat frame down over the legs, guiding the top of each front leg up into the space between the two support strips on one inside surface of the seat frame. The tops of the front legs should be even with the upper edge of the seat frame. The tops of the back legs should be 1¾ inches below the upper edge of the seat frame, and 3½ inches from the back cross-frame member **B**. Glue the legs to the frame members **A** and secure each joint by inserting two of the longer screws through the leg into the frame member.

2. The seat slats run crosswise inside the frame, with their ends resting on the support strips on each side. Glue one of the support strips **I** across the inside surface of one front leg, ¾ inch below the upper end. Secure it by inserting two of the shorter screws through the strip into the leg. Attach the remaining **I** strip to the opposite front leg in the same manner.

3. The three **J** pieces and the two shorter **K** pieces will serve as the seat slats. Place them flat across the frame with the ends resting on the support strips as shown in **Figure M**. The front **J** slat should be about midway between the front frame member **B** and the front legs. The two shorter **K** slats are placed between the front legs, flush with the front and back edges of the legs. The two remaining **J** slats go behind the front legs as shown. Place the first one about 1½ inches from the legs, and the second one about the same distance from the first one. This should leave approximately the same distance again between the last **J** slat and the **B** frame member directly behind it. Be sure that the slats are turned so that each is resting on a wide side, not on edge, and does not extend up past the upper edges of the frame. Secure each end of each slat with glue and one shorter screw inserted down through the slat into the support strip.

4. Refer to **Figure N** as you attach the back assembly to the seat frame. Slide the lower drilled ends of the back section members **E** down inside the seat frame, just behind the center **B** member, and adjust them to align the bolt holes in the **E** pieces with those in the **A** pieces. On each side, insert a bolt from the outside through both pieces and secure it loosely on the inside with a washer and nut. Pivot the back support assembly downward and slide the dowel rod ends into a set of aligned notches in the **A** frame members. It may be necessary to file or plane a little more off the lower ends or lower outer edges of the **O** supports if they will not clear the back **B** frame member.

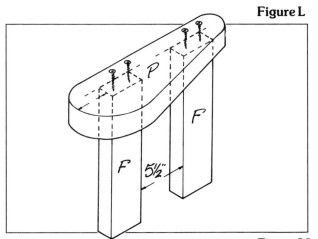

Figure L

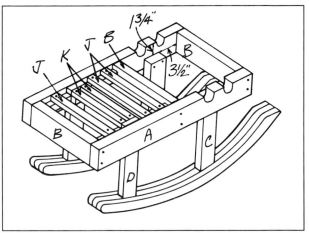

Figure M

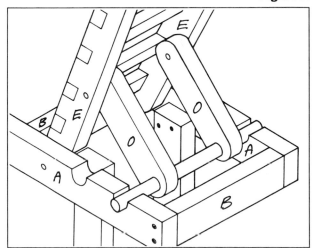

Figure N

Figure O

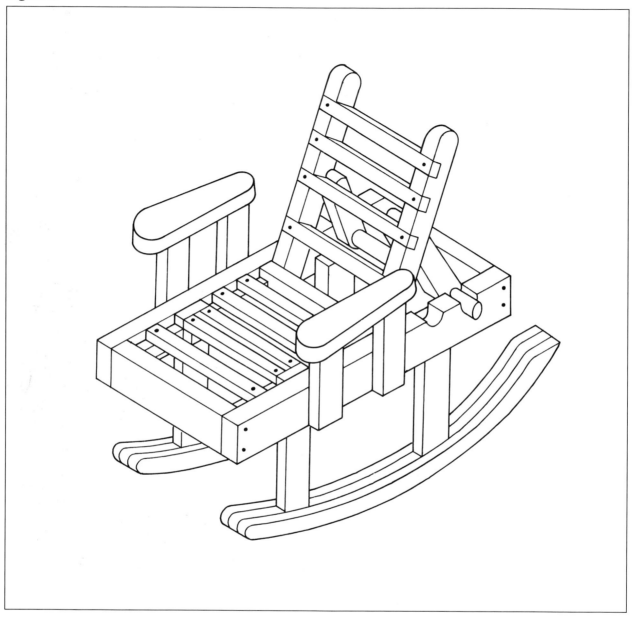

5. The entire assembled rocker is shown in **Figure O**. Glue one arm assembly to the outside of the seat frame, against one of the **A** members, aligning the front armrest support with the front chair leg as shown. The lower ends of the armrest supports should be flush with the lower edge of the **A** frame member. Note that the straight edge of the armrest faces the center. Secure the joints by inserting two long screws through each support into the **A** member. Attach the remaining arm assembly in the same manner.

6. Add the cushion and take your rocker for a long, leisurely test drive.

Footstool

This useful little structure can be built in practically no time at all. You can use it as a footstool, an occasional table (literally), or in a pinch as extra seating space. Overall dimensions are roughly 24 x 14 x 12 inches.

Figure A

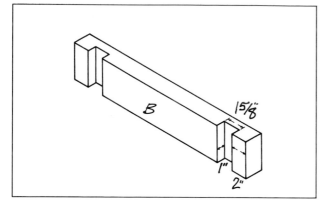

Materials

15 linear feet of 2 x 2 redwood
10 linear feet of 2 x 4 redwood
Twenty-two No. 6 gauge flathead wood screws, each
    2½ inches long; and eight of the same type screws,
    each 1½ inches long

Once the redwood boards are cut to length, even a child could assemble this project. It's basically just a rectangular 2 x 4 frame with the legs attached inside and 2 x 2 slats attached across the top. If there are aspiring young woodworkers in your family, call them in to help with the assembly process.

Cutting the Parts

1. Cut the parts listed below and label each with its identifying code.

Code	Length	Quantity	Material
A	12 inches	2	2 x 4
B	24 inches	2	2 x 4
C	10½ inches	4	2 x 4
D	24 inches	7	2 x 2

2. The B pieces will serve as part of the rectangular frame and must be dadoed to accommodate the A pieces as shown in the assembly diagram, **Figure B**. Cut a 1⅝ x 1-inch dado 2 inches from each end of one B piece. A detail diagram is provided in **Figure A**. Be sure to cut both dadoes across the same side. Dado the remaining B piece in the same manner.

Figure B

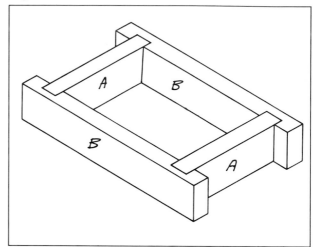

Figure C

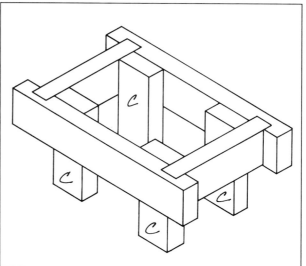

Assembly

1. Assemble the rectangular frame using the A and B pieces, as shown in **Figure B**. Secure each joint with glue and two of the shorter screws inserted through the B piece into the end of the A piece.

2. The C pieces will serve as the legs. Place one leg in each inside corner of the assembled frame, with one side of the leg butted against the B piece and one edge butted against the A piece. The end of the leg should be flush with the upper surfaces of the frame pieces as

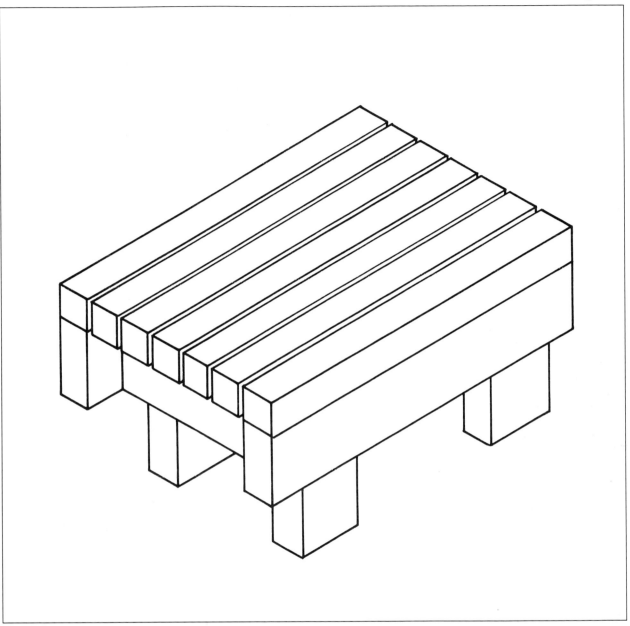

shown in **Figure C**. Secure each leg using glue and two of the longer screws inserted through the leg into the B piece.

3. The D pieces will serve as the slats that form the top of the footstool. Place the slats across the frame as shown in **Figure D**, allowing a ½-inch space between slats. The two outer slats should be even with the outer edges of the frame. Secure each slat using glue and two of the longer screws, one inserted down through the slat and into the frame near each end.

Patio Coffee Table

This convenient little patio table has a two-wheeled frame so it can be moved quite easily. It's also a breeze to make. The circular top is 32 inches in diameter and stands 16 inches tall.

Materials

16 linear feet of 2 x 6 redwood
17 linear feet of 2 x 4 redwood
3 linear feet of 1 x 8 redwood
2-foot length of 1-inch-diameter wooden dowel rod
Forty-four No. 12 gauge flathead wood screws, each
    2½ inches long; and two No. 6 gauge, 1 inch long

Cutting the Parts

1. Cut the parts listed below from the specified materials. Label each part with its identifying code.

Code	Length	Quantity	Material
A	33 inches	2	2 x 6
B	31 inches	2	2 x 6
C	24 inches	2	2 x 6
D	26 inches	2	2 x 4
E	19 inches	4	2 x 4
F	13 inches	1	2 x 4
G	20 inches	2	2 x 4

2. Cut four wheels from the 1 x 8 redwood, each a 6-inch-diameter circle. Glue two of the wheels together, turning them so the grain of one runs perpendicular to the grain of the other. Glue the remaining two wheels together in the same manner. Drill a 1⅛-inch-diameter hole through the exact center of each wheel.

3. The A, B, and C pieces will serve as the tabletop slats, and must be contoured so that they form a circle. Align the slats on a flat surface as shown in **Figure A**. Glue and clamp them together. When the glue has dried, draw the outline of a 32-inch-diameter circle on the slats as shown. To do this, find the center from end to end between the two A pieces and insert a small nail at the center point. Tie a string to the nail and tie a pencil to the opposite end of the string so that the distance between nail and pencil is exactly 16 inches. Now simply pivot the pencil around the nail, keeping the string taut as you draw the circle. Cut the ends of the boards along the outline.

4. The E pieces will serve as the table legs. On two of the E pieces cut a 60-degree miter at each end, as shown in **Figure B**. On the two remaining E pieces cut a 60-degree miter at one end and round off the corners at the opposite end (**Figure C**). Drill a 1-inch-diameter

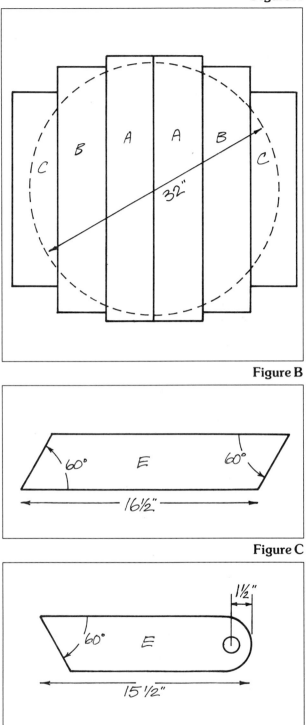

Figure A

Figure B

Figure C

Figure D

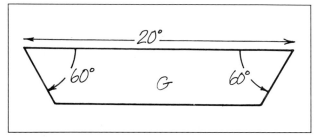

Figure E

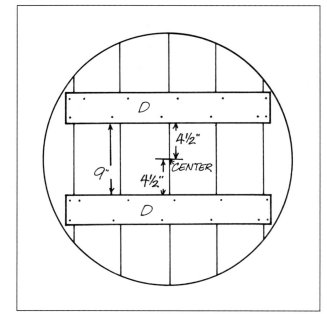

Figure F

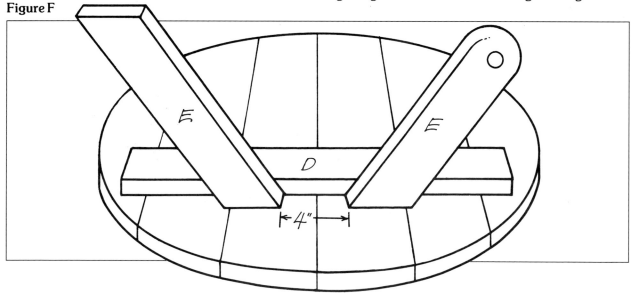

hole through each of the rounded legs, 1½ inches from the rounded end.

5. The G pieces will serve as braces for the table legs. Miter both ends of each brace at a 60-degree angle (**Figure D**).

6. The wheels will be attached using wooden washers and disks. To cut these, you'll need to slice some scrap redwood down to a ¼-inch thickness. From the ¼-inch-thick scrap cut four circular pieces, each 2 inches in diameter. Leave two of the circles as they are – they will serve as the disks. Drill a 1⅛-inch-diameter hole through the center of each remaining circular piece–they will serve as the washers.

Assembly

1. Place the tabletop wrong side up on a flat surface. Place the two D pieces across the slats, allowing 9 inches of space between them (**Figure E**). Note that each brace should be 4½ inches from the center of the tabletop. Glue the braces in place and secure each one using two screws near each end and two screws inserted through the brace into each slat.

2. Place one straight and one rounded leg (E) on the tabletop, against the outer edge of one brace (D) as shown in **Figure F**. Allow 4 inches of space between the legs at the closest point and place the legs equally distant from the center line of the tabletop. Secure each leg using two screws inserted through the leg into the

BUILDING OUTDOOR FURNITURE

D piece. Attach the two remaining legs to the outer edge of the opposite D piece in the same manner. To insure that the rounded legs are aligned properly, slide the length of dowel rod through the holes before you permanently attach the second rounded leg.

3. To make the center brace assembly, glue a mitered G piece to each end of the F piece as shown in **Figure G**. Be sure that the F piece is centered between the ends of each G piece, and secure each joint using two screws.

4. Slide the brace assembly down between the two sets of table legs, and glue it in place as shown in **Figure H** so that the ends of the G pieces are flush with the outer edges of the legs. On each side, secure the brace assembly using two screws inserted through the G piece into each leg.

5. Adjust the dowel rod so that it extends equally beyond each leg. On each end, install a washer and a wheel. The axle should extend slightly beyond the wheels. Place a disk flat against one end of the axle and secure it using one of the short screws. Use the remaining disk to finish the opposite end of the axle.

Figure G

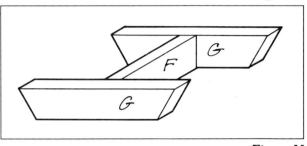

Figure H

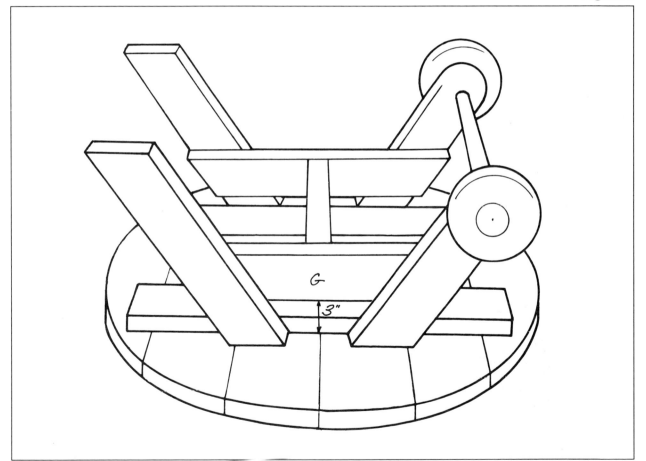

Storage Bench

This handy redwood bench not only seats two people comfortably, but will store a large bag of charcoal, barbecue tongs, a bag of wood chips, and other necessities of lazy living as well. It is one of the most useful pieces of patio furniture we have, and can be constructed in just a couple of hours. Overall dimensions are 39 x 21 x 16 inches. A standard patio chair cushion will fit the bench.

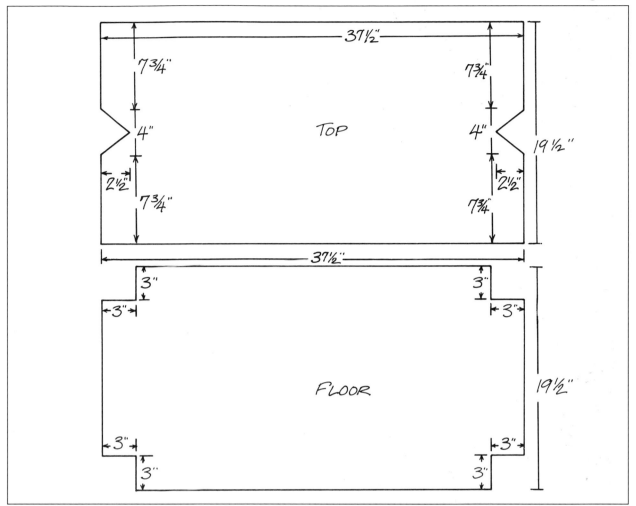

Materials

26 linear feet of 2 x 2 redwood

60 linear feet of 1 x 2 redwood

4 x 4-foot piece of ¾-inch exterior-grade plywood or
    waferwood

Standard patio chair cushion

6d common nails

The storage bench consists of 2 x 2 upper and lower frames and legs, to which slats are nailed on all four sides. The solid floor and top are cut from plywood, and the top is left unsecured so it may be removed.

Cutting the Parts

1. Cut the following parts from 2 x 2 redwood, and label each with its identifying code.

Code	Length	Quantity
A	37½ inches	4
B	16½ inches	4
C	16 inches	4

2. Cut the bench top and floor from plywood or waferwood, making each 37½ x 19½ inches. Each must be modified to fit, as shown in **Figure A**. The

Figure B

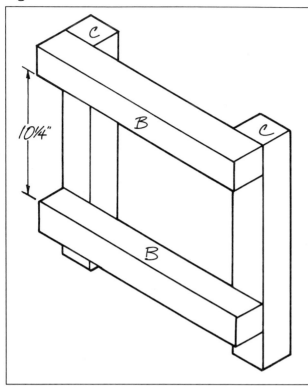

Figure C

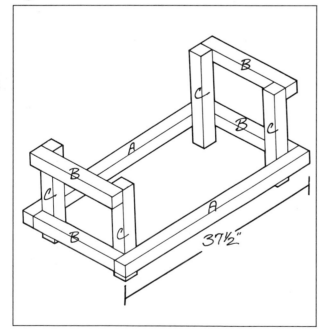

triangular cutouts in the plywood top need not be exact. They will be used simply as handholds to remove the top.

3. Cut forty-six slats from 1 x 2 redwood, each 14 inches long.

Building the Frame

The frame consists of four vertical corner legs, to which horizontal supports are attached at the top and near the bottom. The side slats are simply nailed to these supports.

1. Assemble the ends of the frame first. For each end section, two C pieces will serve as the legs and two B pieces will serve as horizontal supports. Nail two B pieces to two C pieces as shown in **Figure B**. Attach the upper B piece flush with the tops of the legs, and allow 10¼ inches between the upper and lower B pieces. Build a second end section in the same manner using the remaining B and C pieces.

2. Connect the two assembled ends using two A pieces as lower horizontal supports (**Figure C**). The ends of the A pieces should overlap the ends of the lower B pieces.

3. Lay the plywood floor over the lower supports, inside the frame. The corner cutouts will accommodate the corner legs.

4. Attach the remaining two A pieces as upper horizontal supports, flush with the upper edges of the legs.

Adding the Slats

All four sides of the bench frame are covered with slats, which should extend ¾ inch above the upper frame pieces.

1. Begin by nailing seven slats to each end of the frame, spacing them evenly approximately 1 inch apart. Nail each slat to both the top and bottom horizontal supports as shown in **Figure D**.

2. Nail sixteen slats to each side of the frame, overlapping the end slats as shown in **Figure D**.

Finishing

Drop the plywood top inside the frame and place the cushion on top.

BUILDING OUTDOOR FURNITURE

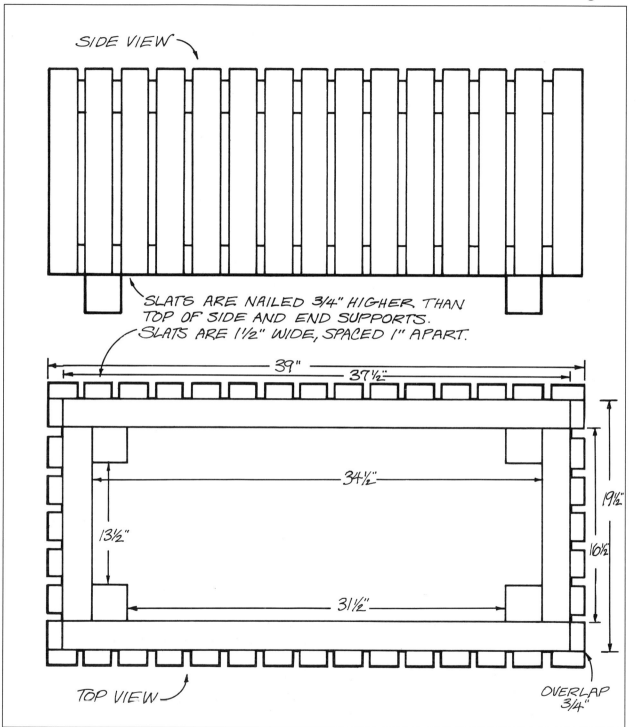

SIDE VIEW

SLATS ARE NAILED 3/4" HIGHER THAN
TOP OF SIDE AND END SUPPORTS.
SLATS ARE 1½" WIDE, SPACED 1" APART.

39"

37½"

34½"

13½"

31½"

19½"

16½"

TOP VIEW

OVERLAP
3/4"

Serving Cart & Tray

This convenient serving cart is trimmed with redwood gingerbread, which makes it a perfect patio-party serving vehicle. The matching tray fits into the cart top, and is removable so it can be used solo. Overall dimensions of the cart are roughly 42 x 18 x 32 inches. The tray is 11 x 24 x 4 inches.

Materials

Redwood: We used the eight different sizes of standard dimensional redwood listed below, which require primarily only cross cuts and very few rip cuts. If you don't mind the extra cutting, you may prefer to re-calculate and purchase only two or three different sizes from which to cut the parts, as you may save a bit of money by doing so. We used:

6 linear feet of 1 x 2 redwood
10 linear feet of 1 x 4 redwood
17 linear feet of 1 x 8 redwood
5 linear feet of 1 x 10 redwood
5 linear feet of 1 x 12 redwood
6 linear feet of 2 x 2 redwood
40 linear feet of 2 x 4 redwood
2 linear feet of 2 x 10 redwood

Wooden dowel rod:

4 feet of 1-inch rod
2 feet of ½-inch rod
3 feet of ⅜-inch rod

Exterior-grade plywood:

2 x 3-foot piece of ¼-inch
3 x 3-foot piece of ⅝-inch

Two metal washers, each 2 inches in diameter with a 1⅛-inch-diameter center hole

Four nail-on rubber cushion-glide casters, each ¾ to 1 inch in diameter

Four ornamental hinges, each about 1½ inches long with flanges no wider than 1½ inches, with screws to fit

Two bolt-type decorative door knobs

Two cabinet catches

16d, 8d, and 4d common and finishing nails

The serving cart consists of an inner frame and top made from 2 x 4 and 2 x 2 stock. The walls are made from 1-inch stock, and the plywood floor extends beyond the cabinet wall on one end to form the open lower shelf. Above this shelf is the extension of the upper frame, which holds the serving tray. The ginger-bread trim is cut from 1-inch stock. Each wheel is a double thickness of plywood, with decorative circular cut-outs made in the outer piece.

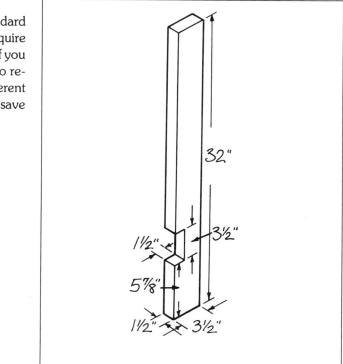

Figure A

Cutting the Parts

1. Cut the parts listed below from redwood 2 x 4 and label each with its identifying code.

Code	Length	Quantity
A	18 inches	8
B	11 inches	2
C	32 inches	2
D	24 inches	2
E	27½ inches	2
F	36½ inches	2
G	15 inches	2

2. The C pieces will serve as the long frame uprights and must be dadoed to accommodate the lower frame members. (The assembled frame is shown in **Figure L**.) Refer to the cutting diagram, **Figure A**, as you cut a dado across one edge of each C piece, making the dado 1½ inches deep, 3½ inches long, and 5⅞ inches from one end of the leg. This will be the lower end.

Figure B

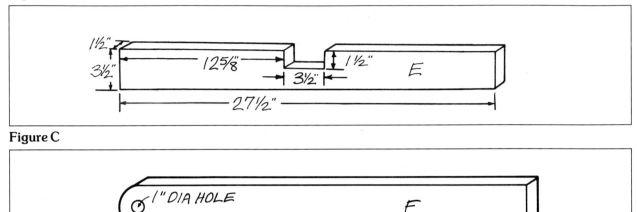

Figure C

3. The E pieces will serve as the lower frame members and must be dadoed to accommodate the shorter uprights. Refer to the cutting diagram provided in **Figure B** as you cut a dado across one edge of each E piece, making the dado 1½ inches deep, 3½ inches long, and 12⅝ inches from one end.

4. The F pieces will serve as the upper frame members. Refer to the cutting diagram provided in **Figure C** as you round off the corners at one end of one F piece, and drill a 1-inch-diameter hole 1¾ inches from the rounded end. Use the contoured and drilled F piece as a pattern to contour and drill the remaining F piece so the holes will be perfectly aligned.

5. Cut the parts listed below from redwood 1 x 8 and label each with its identifying code.

Code	Length	Quantity
H	15 inches	2
I	24¾ inches	2
J	20½ inches	2
K	11½ inches	2

6. Enlarge the scale drawing for the tray side L provided in **Figure D**, and cut two tray sides from the remaining 1 x 8 redwood. Drill two ½-inch-diameter holes through one tray side where indicated on the drawing. Use the drilled tray side as a guide to drill the

holes in the second tray side so they will be aligned perfectly. Label each tray side L.

7. A scale drawing for the shelf end trim H is also provided in **Figure D**. Enlarge the drawing and contour one long edge of each of the two H pieces that you cut in step 5.

8. The two K pieces will serve as the shelf side trim. Enlarge the scale drawing provided in **Figure D** and contour both K pieces that you cut in step 5. Drill a 1⅛-inch-diameter hole through one K piece where indicated on the scale drawing. The hole will accommodate the axle. Use the drilled K piece as a guide to drill the other K piece, so the holes will be aligned.

9. Cut the parts listed below from the designated materials and label each part with its identifying code.

Code	Length	Quantity	Material
M	12 inches	1	2 x 2
N	15 inches	2	2 x 2
O	22¾ inches	2	1 x 12
P	23 inches	2	1 x 2
Q	9¼ inches	2	1 x 2
R	23 inches	2	1 x 10
S	10¾ inches	2	1 x 4
T	19½ inches	4	1 x 4
U	14¾ inches	1	2 x 10
V	11 inches	2	2 x 2

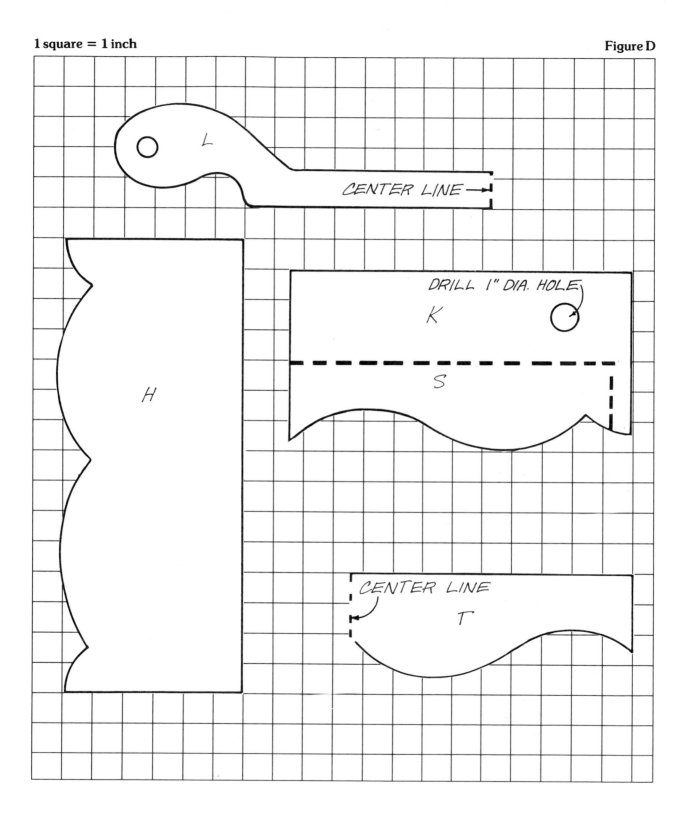

L

CENTER LINE →

DRILL 1" DIA. HOLE

K

S

H

CENTER LINE

T

Figure E

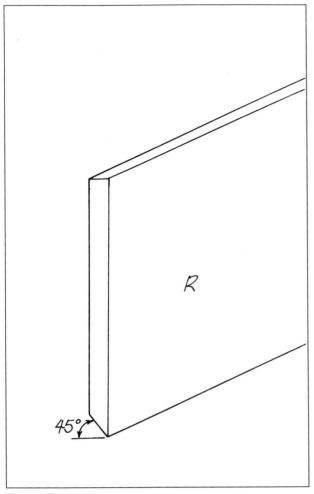

$45°$

R

10. The two O pieces will serve as the panels that form the back wall of the cabinet. (For reference, we have designated the side of the cart with the cabinet doors as the front, and the opposite side as the back.) Overall dimensions of the back wall are 19½ x 22¾ inches. Trim each of the O pieces down to a width of 9¾ inches so that when they are placed side by side against the frame they will make up the proper width. Do not alter the length of either board.

11. The two R pieces will serve as the doors on the front of the cabinet. Trim each R piece down to a width of 8⅛ inches, but do not alter the length. We beveled one long edge of each door (what will be the center edge) to make them fit together properly yet close and open easily. Bevel one long edge of each R piece at a 45-degree angle as shown in **Figure E**.

12. The S pieces will serve as the upper side trim at the shelf end of the cart. Contour one long edge of each S piece using the pattern you made for the shelf side trim K.

13. The T pieces will serve as the upper and lower trim on the cabinet front and back. Enlarge the scale drawing for the T trim provided in **Figure D**, and cut the contour along one long edge of each of the four T pieces. The two T trim pieces that will be attached to the cabinet back will be used as they are. The two that will be attached to the cabinet front must be cut into separate sections to accommodate the doors. Cut two of the T trim pieces into four sections each as shown in the cutting diagram, **Figure F**.

Figure F

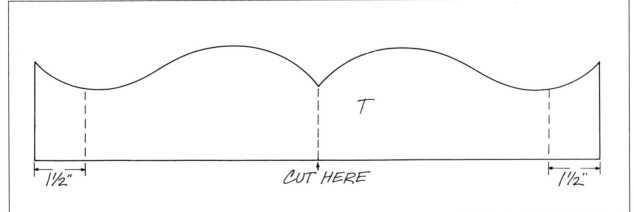

1½"   CUT HERE   T   1½"

14. The wheels are cut from ⅝-inch plywood. Cut four circular wheels, each 14½ inches in diameter, and cut or drill a 1⅛-inch-diameter hole through the center of each one. Each finished wheel will consist of two of these pieces glued together. We made decorative circular cutouts in two of the pieces, and used them as the outer pieces. A cutting diagram showing the circular cutouts is provided in **Figure G**. Make the cutouts in only two of the plywood wheels.

15. Cut two wooden washers, each 2¼ inches in diameter, from ⅝-inch plywood. Cut or drill a 1⅛-inch-diameter hole through the center of each one.

16. The cabinet floor extends out beyond the wall at the wheel end of the cart to form the open shelf. Cut one floor from ¼-inch plywood, 15 x 29¾ inches. The floor must be notched to accommodate the frame members. Cut four rectangular notches in the floor as shown in **Figure H**, using the same measurements on both sides.

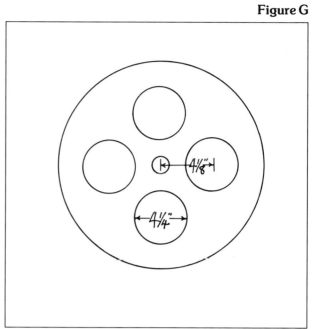

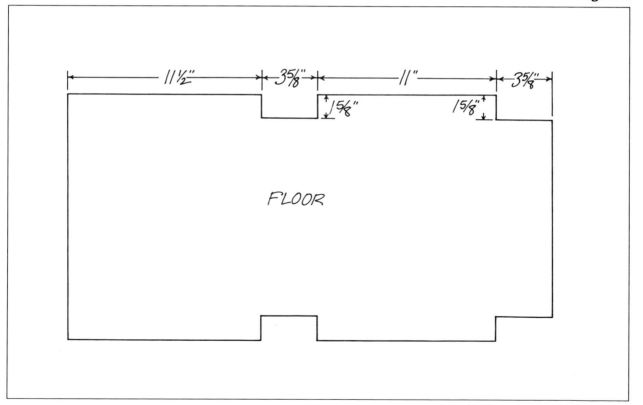

FLOOR

Figure I

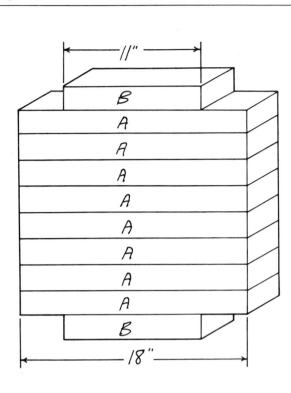

Figure J

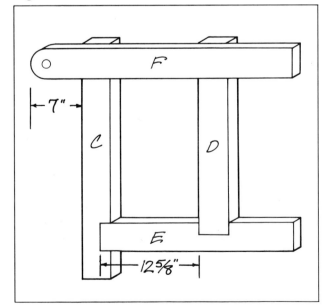

Figure K

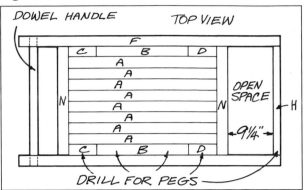

Building the Frame

Note: Secure all joints with glue and nails unless otherwise specified.

1. The eight A pieces and two B pieces form the cart top. Place the eight A pieces side by side, on edge, as shown in **Figure I**. Place one B piece next to each outer A piece as shown, centering them between the ends. Glue the boards together and clamp them overnight.

2. The frame consists of two identical side sections. To make one side section, join one C, one D, one E, and one F piece as shown in **Figure J**. Be sure that the E piece is turned the right way end for end, as shown, because the dado that accommodates the upright D piece is slightly closer to one end than to the other. The upper edge of the F piece should be flush with the upper ends of the C and D uprights. Use the remaining C, D, E, and F pieces to construct an identical side section, making it a mirror image of the first one by placing the F piece against the opposite side.

3. Cut an 18-inch length of 1-inch dowel to serve as the handle. Place the two frame sides about 15 inches apart and glue the following pieces between them as shown in the top view drawing, **Figure K**: the dowel handle, the assembled cart top with an N piece at each end, and one H trim piece. Note that the upper ends of the C and D frame uprights fill the gaps between the shorter B pieces of the cart top and the crosswise N pieces. The upper edges and ends of all these pieces should be flush, and the straight upper edge of the H trim should be flush with the upper edges of the F frame members. The ends of the dowel handle are inserted

Figure L

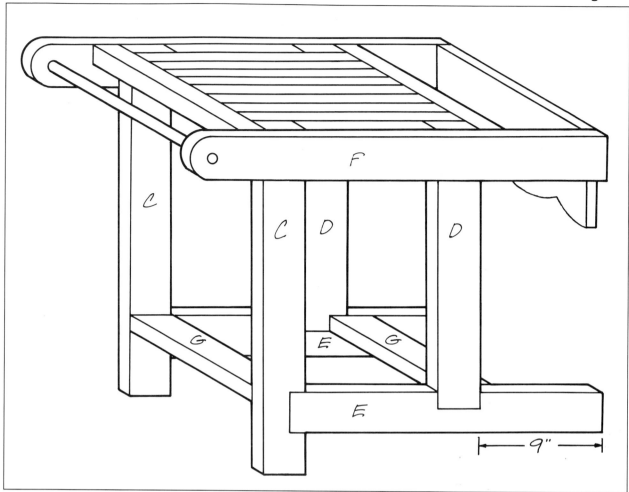

into the holes in the F frame members. We used pegs instead of nails to secure this assembly. Cut ten pegs from ⅜-inch dowel rod, each 2¼ inches long. Drill five peg sockets, each 2¼ inches deep, into each side of the assembly where indicated in **Figure K**, midway between the upper and lower edges of the frame F pieces. Glue a peg into each hole and trim the ends flush with the F members. Use nails to secure the crosswise N pieces to the ends of the cart-top boards.

4. The two G pieces serve as cross braces connecting the two frame sides near the bottom as shown in **Figure L**. Glue one G piece between the two frame uprights C. The upper side of the G piece should be flush with the upper edges of the E frame members. Glue the second G piece between the two E members 9 inches from the open end of the frame as shown. Again, the upper side of the G piece should be flush with the upper edges of the E members.

5. Now lay the plywood floor in place and glue and nail it to the E and G pieces.

6. The two V pieces will serve as braces. Glue one V piece to the lower edge of one B cart-top board, between the frame uprights C and D. Secure it by driving a couple of nails up through it into the B board. Attach the remaining V piece to the lower edge of the B board on the opposite side of the cart.

SERVING CART & TRAY

Figure M

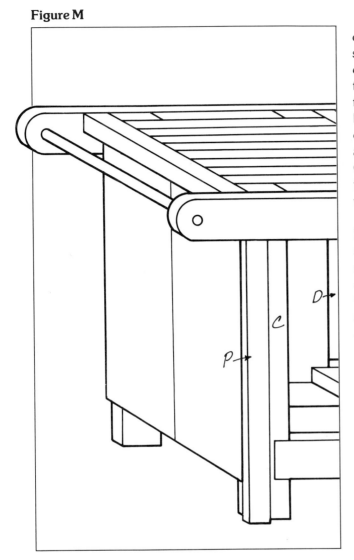

Building the Cabinet

1. The two I pieces serve as the cabinet wall panels at the handle end of the cart. Place them side by side against the frame. The upper ends of the I panels should butt up against the bottom of the N piece that runs across the end of the cart top, and the outer edges of the panels should be even with the outer sides of the frame uprights C. Glue and nail the panels to the ends of the cart-top boards, to the edges of the C uprights, and to the edge of the lower cross brace G.

2. The two J pieces serve as the wall panels at the opposite (shelf) end of the cabinet. Place them side by side against the frame uprights D, butting the upper ends against the bottom of the N piece that runs across that end of the cart top. Glue and nail the J panels to the ends of the cart-top boards and to the edges of the D uprights. The lower ends of the J panels should rest on the plywood floor. The 2 x 2 M piece will serve as a brace at the bottom of this wall, inside the cabinet. Glue and nail the M piece to the plywood floor and to the lower ends of the J panels, on the side facing the wall already in place at the handle end.

3. The two O pieces serve as the wall panels for the back of the cabinet. Place them side by side against one side of the frame (we chose the left-hand side, if you are standing at the handle end of the cart). The upper ends of the O panels should be butted snugly against the bottom of the F frame member, and the panels should cover the edges of the two walls already in place so that the outer edges of the panels are even with the outer sides of these two walls. Glue and nail the panels to the edges of the other two walls, to the C and D frame uprights, to the V brace between the C and D uprights at the top, and to the lower frame member E.

4. The remaining side of the cabinet consists of the two doors R and two facers P shown in **Figure N**. Place one P facer against the remaining open side of the frame as shown in **Figure M**, so that the upper end is butted firmly against the bottom of the F frame member. The facer should cover the edge of the end wall, so that the outer edge of the facer is even with the outside surface of the wall. Glue and nail the facer to the edge of the wall and to the frame upright C. Attach the remaining facer P to the frame upright D and to the edge of the wall at that end of the cabinet.

5. The door trim must be added before the doors can be hinged in place. Use the two T trims that you cut into separate pieces. Glue and nail the trim in place, positioning the lower trim pieces 2¾ inches above the lower edges of the doors and facers as shown in **Figure N**. The upper trim pieces should be placed about ⅛ inch below the upper edges of the doors and facers. Hinge the doors to the facers, placing the hinges on top of the trim pieces as shown in **Figure N**. Install the two door knobs and install the cabinet catches inside.

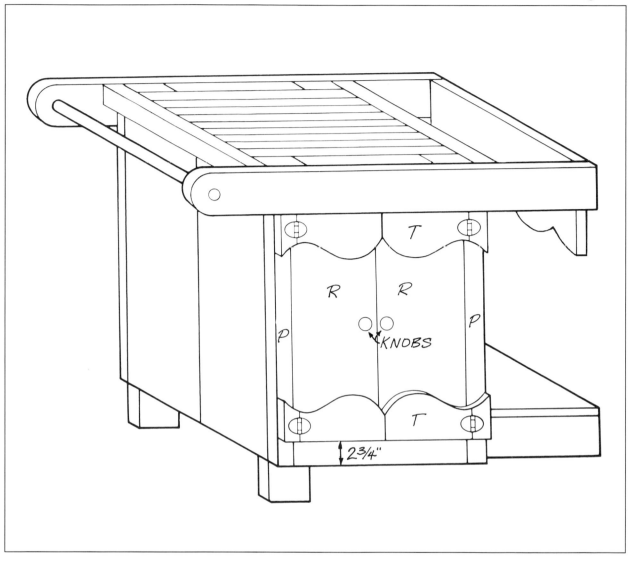

Adding the Trim and Wheels

1. Attach the two undivided T pieces to the back wall of the cabinet, butting the upper trim piece against the lower edge of the frame F piece, and placing the lower trim piece 3 inches above the lower edge of the wall.

2. Glue and nail the two K trim pieces to the sides of the shelf as shown in **Figure O**. The straight lower edge of each trim piece should be flush with the lower edge of the cabinet wall against which the trim is butted. Glue and nail the remaining H trim piece to the end of the shelf and to the ends of the E frame members, between the K trims as shown.

3. Before the axle can be inserted, the E frame members must be drilled to accommodate it. On each side of the frame, drill a hole through the E member, using the hole in the K trim as a guide. Drill in as straight a line as possible or the axle will not fit.

Figure O

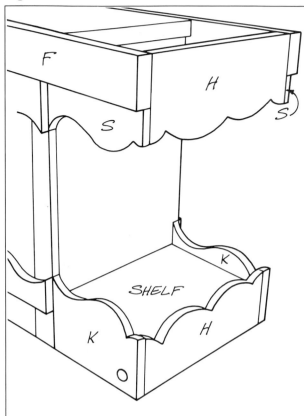

Figure P

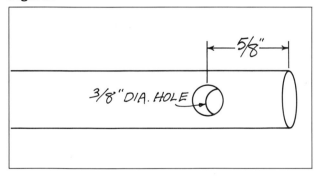

Figure Q

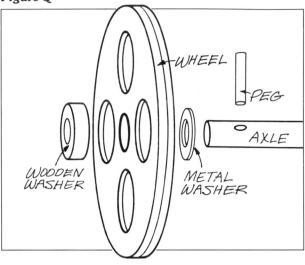

be driven through the **S** trim into this block for extra strength. The **S** trim should cover the end of the **H** trim piece where it extends below the **F** frame member. Drive a couple of finishing nails through the **S** trim into the end of the **H** trim. Attach the remaining **S** trim to the opposite side of the frame in the same manner.

5. To make one finished wheel glue together two plywood wheel pieces, one with decorative cutouts and one without, making sure the center holes are aligned. Use wood filler to fill the grain around the outer edge of the wheel, and lubricate the center hole with beeswax or hard soap. Assemble a second wheel in the same manner.

6. Cut a 22¼-inch length of 1-inch dowel for the axle. Drill a ⅜-inch-diameter hole straight through the axle, placing the center of the hole ⅝ inch from one end (**Figure P**). Repeat the drilling procedure at the opposite end of the axle. Insert the axle through the axle holes in the cart, leaving equal extensions on each side. Glue the axle in place.

7. The wheel installation is shown in **Figure Q**. At each end of the axle install a metal washer, a wheel (cutout side facing outward), and a wooden washer. Cut a 2¼-inch length of ⅜-inch dowel to serve as a holding pin and insert it through the hole near the end of the axle.

8. Nail two rubber cushion-glide casters to the bottom of each **C** frame upright.

4. On one side of the frame, glue one **S** trim piece to the lower edge of the **F** frame member as shown in **Figure O**. The inside surface of the trim should be flush with the inside surface of the **F** member. We cut a small support block and attached it to the cabinet end wall in the corner created by the **S** trim. A couple of nails can

BUILDING OUTDOOR FURNITURE

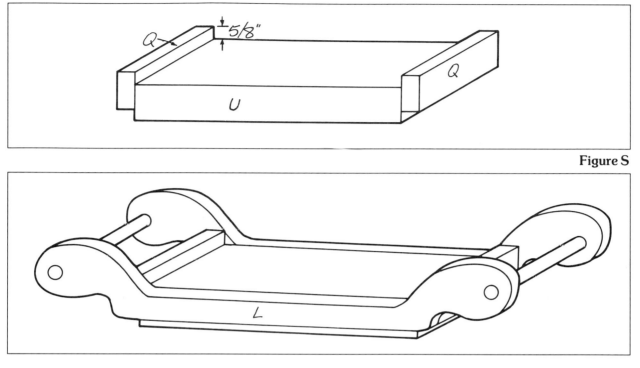

9. We added three hanger pegs to the handle end of the cart top to accommodate hanging utensils, pot holders and the like. If you wish to add hanger pegs, first drill three sockets, each ⅜ inch in diameter and ½ inch deep, into the vertical edge of the N piece that runs across the end of the cart top at the handle end of the cart. Drill at a slight downward angle so the pegs will slant upward. Cut three 1¾-inch-long pegs from ⅜-inch dowel and cut one end of each peg at a slight angle so it will seat squarely in the slanted socket. Glue the pegs into the sockets.

Making the Tray

Our serving tray is a bit different than most normal trays. The tray floor extends down below the sides and ends so that it will fit into the opening in the cart frame, while the sides and ends keep it from slipping through.

1. Begin by glueing the two tray ends Q along the ends of the tray floor U as shown in **Figure R**. Note that the tray ends extend up above the top of the floor piece about ⅝ inch. This forms a lip on each end to help keep the goodies from sliding off the tray. Secure the ends with nails.

2. You have already contoured and drilled the two tray sides L. Glue one tray side along one edge of the tray floor as shown in **Figure S**, so that the lower edge of the tray side is even with the lower edges of the tray ends. Secure the tray side with nails. Do not attach the second tray side just yet.

3. Cut two 10¾-inch lengths of ½-inch dowel rod to serve as the tray handles. Insert one handle into the hole at one end of the attached tray side, and insert the other handle into the hole at the opposite end. Place the second tray side against the open edge of the tray floor, inserting the free ends of the dowel handles into the holes in this tray side. Glue and nail the tray side in place and trim the dowel handles if they extend out past the tray sides. Glue the handle ends in place.

4. Lower the tray into the opening at the wheel end of the upper cart frame. If it is a little too snug to slide in and out easily, sand or plane the edges and/or ends of the tray floor where they extend below the tray side and end pieces.

Pyramid Planter

Just 27 inches square at the base and roughly 4 feet tall, this redwood planter provides a beautiful method for growing plants and flowers in a very small space. Trailing plants are particularly delightful, as they will cascade down the sides of the planter.

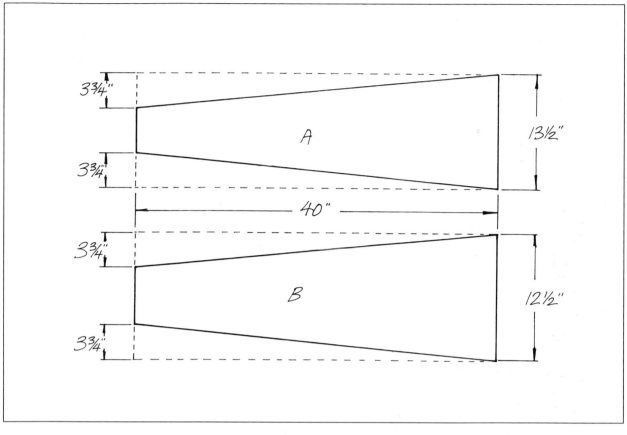

Materials

1 linear foot of 1 x 8 redwood (no waste allowance is
  included)
114 linear feet of 1 x 4 redwood
18 linear feet of 2 x 2 redwood
4 x 4-foot piece of $\frac{7}{16}$-inch waferwood or $\frac{1}{2}$-inch ex-
  terior- grade plywood
4 x 6-foot piece of $\frac{3}{4}$-inch exterior-grade plywood
Four flat-plate swiveling casters, each approximately 3
  inches in diameter
2d galvanized common nails
4d and 6d galvanized finishing nails

The planter consists of a inner pyramid and an outer
frame. Planter boxes are fitted over the frame to provide growing space. Set on casters, the pyramid can be
turned to take advantage of the light.

Constructing the Interior Pyramid

The center of the pyramid is hollow in order to re-
duce the amount of dirt required, and thus the total
weight. The interior pyramid is constructed from waferwood and consists of four sides, a top, and a bottom.

1. Cut the following pieces from $\frac{7}{16}$-inch waferwood
or $\frac{1}{2}$-inch plywood and label each part with its identifying code.

Code	Dimensions	Quantity
A	13½ x 40 inches	2
B	12½ x 40 inches	2
C	6 x 6 inches	1
D	13½ x 13½ inches	1

2. Modify pieces A and B as shown in **Figure A**.

Figure B

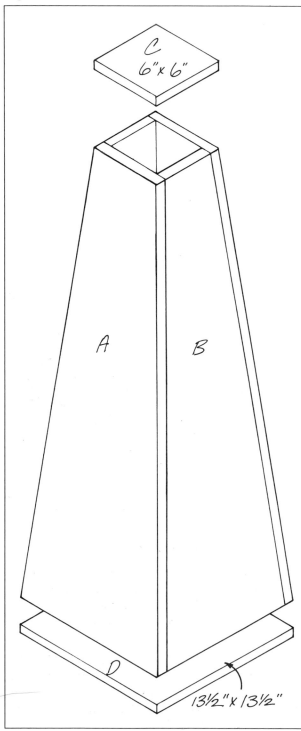

C
6" x 6"

A

B

D

13½" x 13½"

Figure C

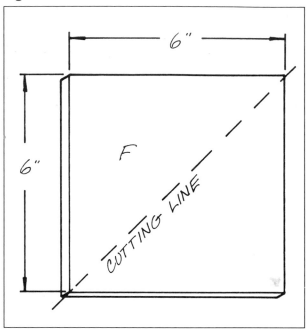

6"

6"

F

CUTTING LINE

3. Nail and glue the **A** pieces over the edges of the B pieces as shown in **Figure B.**

4. Nail and glue the **C** piece over the top of the four-sided pyramid.

5. Nail and glue the **D** piece over the bottom of the pyramid.

Constructing the Base

The weight of the completed pyramid rests on a flat base assembly consisting of upper and lower base pieces. Casters are attached to all four corners of the lower base, which are reinforced with corner supports.

1. Cut a 27-inch-square lower base piece (**E**) from ¾-inch plywood.

2. Cut four reinforcing corner supports (**F**) from 1 x 8 redwood. To cut the triangles, first cut two 6-inch squares. Draw a line connecting opposite corners as shown in **Figure C**, and cut along the line. Nail a triangular support to each of the four corners of the lower base as shown in **Figure D.**

3. Cut a 25½-inch-square upper base (**G**) from ¾-inch plywood. Notch each of the four corners as shown in **Figure E.**

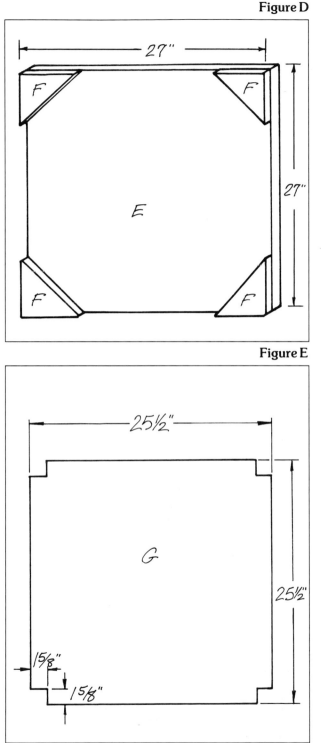

Figure E

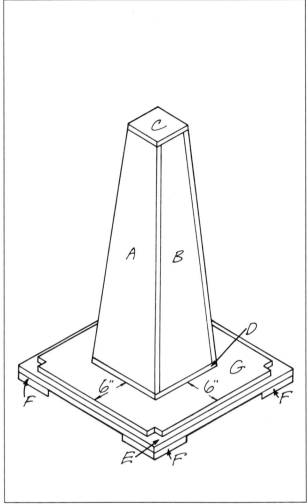

Completing the Frame

The outer planter boxes rest on a frame that is constructed around the interior pyramid. The frame is composed of four 2 x 2 braces attached to the base at the bottom, and a plywood square that connects the braces at the top.

1. Place the lower base (E) on a flat surface. Nail the upper base to the center of the lower base. Place the interior pyramid in the center of the upper base, allowing a 6-inch border on all four sides. Nail and glue the interior pyramid in place (**Figure F**).

Figure G

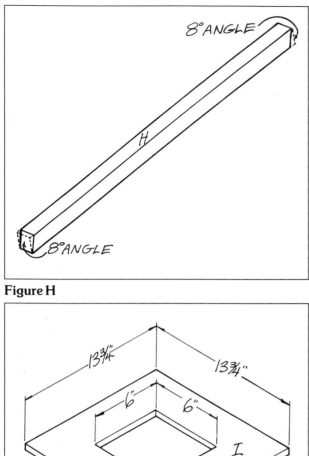

Figure H

Figure I

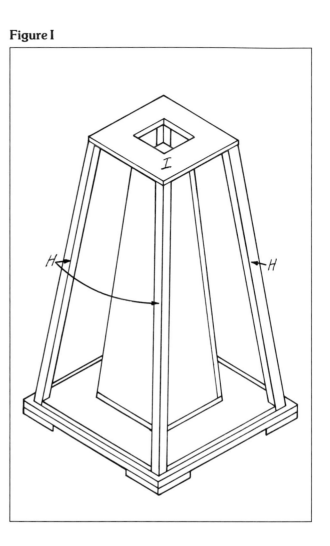

5. Nail the corners of the frame top (I) to the tops of the braces as shown in **Figure I**.

6. Cut two inner support pieces from scrap wood, each approximately 10 inches long, and use them to connect the top of the interior pyramid to the hole in the top of the frame on opposite sides.

Constructing the Planter Boxes

The outside of the pyramid consists of six planter boxes – largest at the bottom, and smallest at the top. Each box is held in place by four support boards nailed directly to the 2 x 2 braces. The box supports are constructed first.

2. Cut four braces (H) from 2 x 2 redwood, each 45¼ inches long. Miter both ends of each brace at an 8-degree angle, as shown in **Figure G**.

3. Cut a frame top (I) from ¾-inch exterior plywood, 13¾ inches square. Cut a 6-inch-square hole in the center as shown in **Figure H**.

4. Fit one end of each 2 x 2 brace into one of the square corner notches in the upper plywood base. Turn each brace so that the top leans toward the center as shown in **Figure I**, and nail it in place at the bottom.

1. Dimensions of the parts required to build the supports and planter boxes are provided below. Each box requires four supports: two long and two short. Cut from 1 x 4 redwood the required supports for Boxes #2 through #6.

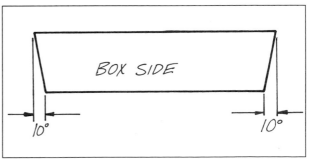

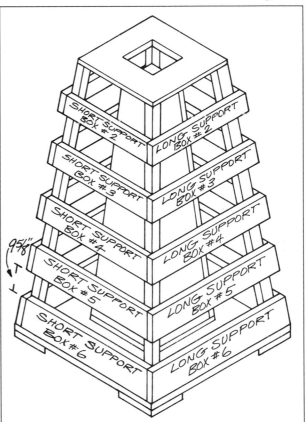

BOX SUPPORT

8°   8°

SHORT SUPPORT BOX #2   LONG SUPPORT BOX #2
SHORT SUPPORT BOX #3   LONG SUPPORT BOX #3
SHORT SUPPORT BOX #4   LONG SUPPORT BOX #4
9⅝″
SHORT SUPPORT BOX #5   LONG SUPPORT BOX #5
SHORT SUPPORT BOX #6   LONG SUPPORT BOX #6

Figure L

BOX SIDE

10°   10°

	Box Supports		Box Sides		
Box#	Long Side	Short Side	Long Sides	Short Sides	Box Bottom
1			14⅛″	12¼″	13″x 13″
2	17″	15½″	22⅝″	21⅛″	21⅝″
3	19½″	18″	25″	23½″	24″
4	22″	20½″	27¾″	26¼″	26½″
5	24½″	23″	30⅛″	28⅝″	29″
6	27″	25½″	32⅞″	31⅜″	31½″

Note: All dimensions in inches.

2. Miter each end of each box support at an 8-degree angle as shown in **Figure J**.

3. Refer to **Figure K** as you attach the box supports to the frame. Begin by nailing the short supports for Box #6 to opposite sides of the 2 x 2 frame, placing the long edge against the pyramid base.

4. Next, nail the long supports for Box #6 to the remaining opposite sides of the 2 x 2 frame, again placing the long edge against the base. The long supports should overlap the ends of the short supports.

5. Measure 9⅝ inches vertically up the 2 x 2 frame and mark this point. This is the placement line for the lower edges of the Box #5 supports. Attach them to the 2 x 2 frame as you did the previous supports. Repeat these procedures to attach the supports for Boxes #4 through #2.

6. Each planter box consists of two short sides and two long sides. Box #1, which sits on top of the pyramid, has a solid plywood floor. Boxes #2 through #6 have floors that are open in the center to fit over the 2 x 2 frame. Refer to the dimensions given in step 1, and cut from 1 x 4 redwood two long sides and two short sides for each box. Miter each end of each box side at a 10-degree angle as shown in **Figure L**. Label each of the pieces.

Figure M

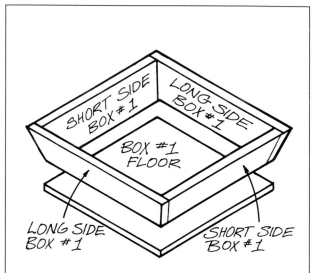

Figure N

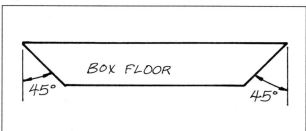

Figure O

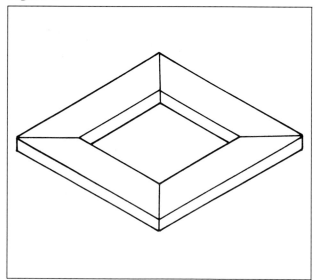

Figure P

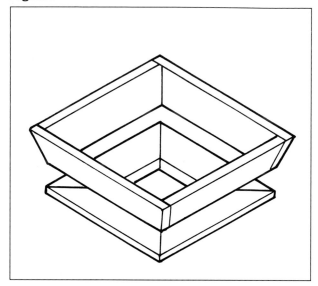

7. Cut a solid box floor for Box #1 from ¾-inch plywood, according to dimensions given in step 1.

8. Assemble Box #1 as shown in **Figure M**, lapping the long sides over the ends of the short sides.

9. Cut from 1 x 4 redwood four box floor pieces for each of Boxes #2 through #6, using the lengths given in step 1. Label the pieces. Miter both ends of each piece at a 45-degree angle as shown in **Figure N**.

10. Nail and glue together the four mitered floor pieces for Box #2 as shown in **Figure O**.

11. Attach the two long sides and two short sides for Box #2 to the completed floor frame as shown in **Figure P**. The long sides should overlap the ends of the short sides as shown.

12. Repeat the procedures in steps 10 and 11 to assemble Boxes #3 through #6.

Finishing

1. Attach the swiveling casters to the reinforcing corner supports on the bottom of the planter.

2. Slip the assembled boxes over the 2 x 2 frame, beginning with Box #6 and ending with Box #2. Refer to **Figure Q**. Place Box #1 on top of the pyramid.

3. Fill the planter with a mixture of potting soil and vermiculite. This will cut down on total weight and provide drainage for the plants.

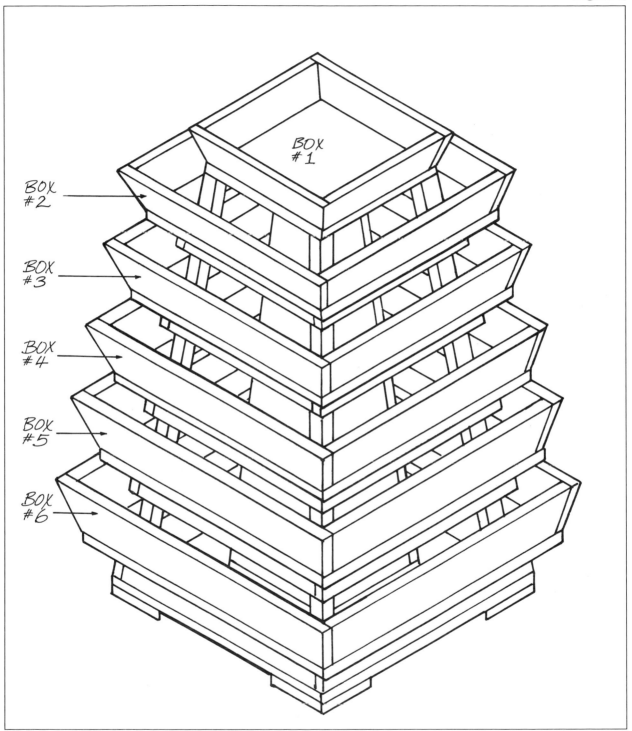

BOX
#1

BOX
#2

BOX
#3

BOX
#4

BOX
#5

BOX
#6

I Love My Planter/Trellis

This unique planter and trellis combination incorporates some unusual construction techniques as well as design features. The trellis is supported by a simple frame connected to the planter floor, and may be removed quite easily. You might wish to plant the trellis in the ground and use the double-tiered planter elsewhere. The planter is 2 feet long, 1½ feet deep, and about 15 inches high. The trellis is roughly 8 feet tall.

Materials

Note: There is a considerable amount of rip-cutting required for the trellis portion of this project. In addition, we employed some unusual (but not difficult if you have the right tools) cutting techniques in building the planter portion. We suggest that you read through the instructions so you'll know what's required before you purchase any materials.

For the trellis:

The body of the trellis is made from either an 8-foot or 10-foot length of redwood 2 x 6, depending on whether you want to plant it or mount it in the planter box. Purchase the shorter board for use with the planter box, or the longer board if you are going to plant the trellis.

3-foot length of knot-free 2 x 6 redwood

8-foot length of 1 x 2 redwood

One ¼ x 6 roundhead stove bolt with a flat washer and nut to fit

½-inch galvanized staples

For the planter box:

14 linear feet of 1 x 3 redwood

14 linear feet of 1 x 8 redwood

1-foot length of 1 x 2 scrap redwood or other wood

3-foot length of 2 x 2 scrap redwood or other wood

2 x 3-foot piece of ¾-inch waferwood or exterior-grade plywood

2 x 2-foot piece of ¼-inch waferwood or exterior-grade plywood

4d finishing nails

This is a two-in-one project, as we said earlier. You may make either or both of the structures, and use them together or separately. We're so fond of the planter that we made several.

THE TRELLIS

The trellis is made by ripping a 5-foot portion of the 8- or 10-foot redwood 2 x 6 into fifteen separate thin ribs, leaving the lower portion of the board uncut so that the ribs are still connected at the bottom. The heart-shaped insert is cut in fourteen sections, which are glued between the trellis ribs. The upper ends of the ribs are fanned outward by spacer slats.

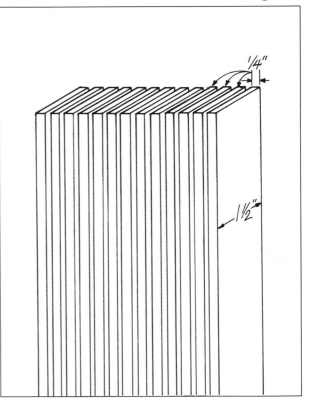

Cutting the Parts

1. Begin by making the required rip cuts in the long 2 x 6 as shown in **Figure A**, to create the trellis ribs. Start at the same end each time and make fourteen passes into the table saw to divide a 5-foot portion of the board into fifteen separate ribs, each ¼ inch thick. Because the width of each saw cut will be ⅛ inch, this should divide the board evenly. If you are using a 10-foot board, this will leave half the length of the board uncut. If you are using an 8-foot board, you'll have a 3-foot-long solid section below the rip cuts. It may seem obvious, but we'll say it anyway: Do not cut across the board to separate the ribs from the lower solid portion of the board. Don't worry about making the ends of the rip cuts neat and clean where they are stopped at the top of the solid portion of the board, because they will be covered later. Do try to make them relatively even across the board.

Figure B

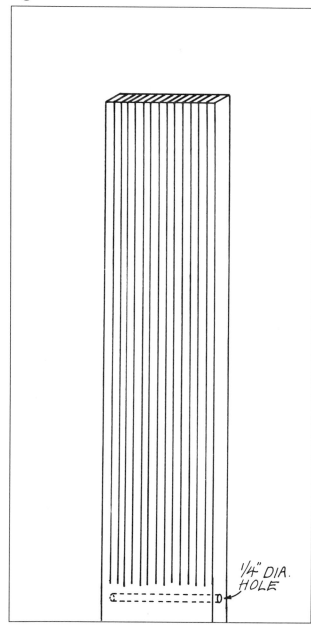

¼" DIA. HOLE

C ----------- D

2. The stove bolt will serve to reinforce the trellis board below the rip cuts, to help keep it from splitting. Drill a ¼-inch-diameter hole all the way through the board from edge to edge, about an inch below the stopped ends of the rip cuts (**Figure B**).

3. A scale drawing for one-half of the heart-shaped insert is provided in **Figure C**. As you can see, the insert is not cut as a solid piece but rather as separate sections. The sections are inserted as spacers between the trellis ribs, and the ribs in turn serve as fillers between the heart sections, giving the overall illusion of a solid heart-shaped insert. (You can see the effect in the photograph and also in the assembly diagram, **Figure E**.) Enlarge the scale drawing to make a full-size pattern for each of the seven heart sections, and cut two of each piece from the knot-free redwood 2 x 6. Label each piece with the code letter provided on the scale drawing, to facilitate assembly later on.

4. When the trellis is assembled, the upper ends of the ribs will be fanned outward and held in place by short spacer slats in between and by one long upper slat on top. To create these pieces, begin by twice ripping the redwood 1 x 2 along the entire length to produce two 8-foot-long slats, each ¼ inch thick and 1½ inches wide. Trim one of these pieces to an overall length of 89 inches. This will serve as the upper slat. From the remaining long slat cut fourteen 6-inch lengths. These will serve as the spacer slats.

5. As we said before, the stopped ends of the trellis rip cuts will be covered. To create the covers, first rip some of the leftover redwood stock to a thickness of ¼ inch. From the ¼-inch material cut two covers, each 3 x 5½ inches.

Assembly

1. To begin, insert the stove bolt into the hole that you drilled through the trellis board. Secure it with a flat washer and nut.

2. Glue one of the redwood covers to one side of the trellis board so that it conceals the stopped ends of the rip cuts (**Figure D**). Glue the remaining cover to the opposite side of the board, even with the first cover. Secure the covers with staples.

3. Insert the fourteen heart sections between the trellis ribs as shown in **Figure E**, adjusting them so that the lower point of the heart appears to be about 5½ inches above the covers. Do not use glue or fasteners to secure the heart sections just yet.

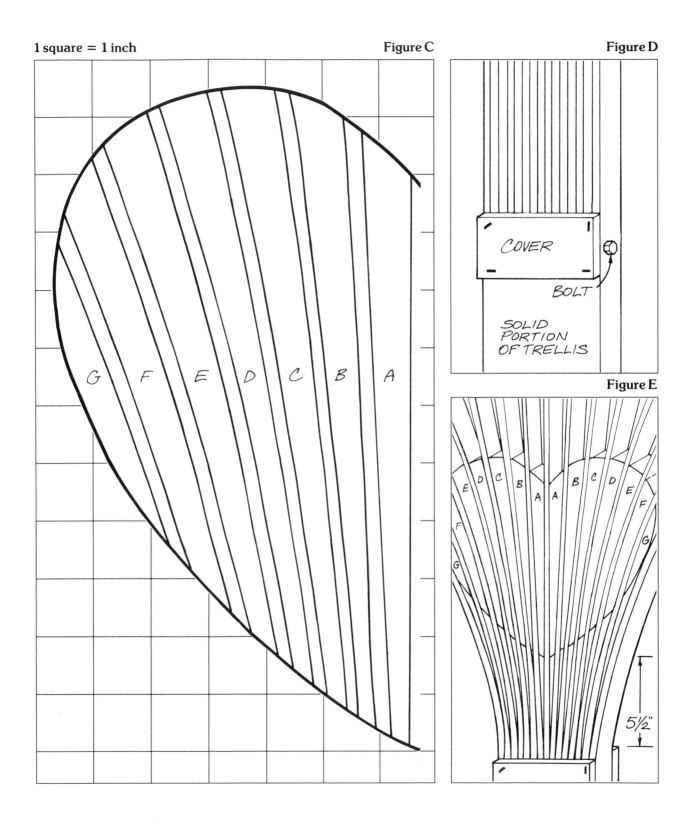

Figure F

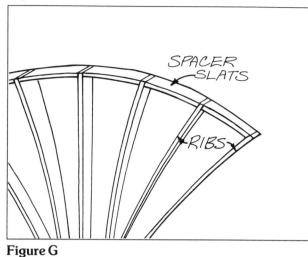

Figure G

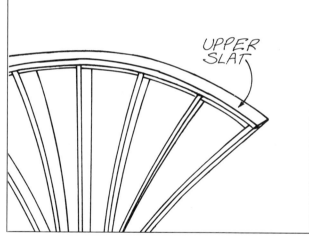

Figure H

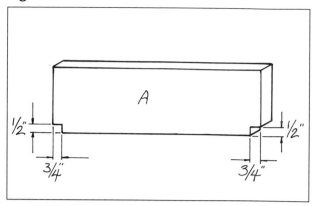

THE PLANTER

The planter appears to be a two-tiered box, but "appears" is the operative word here. There are indeed two tiers of walls, but only the lower, larger box has a floor. This makes for an interesting design, and when the box is filled with dirt the upper walls do provide a second level of growing space. The trim around the upper edges of the walls is attached at an angle, which makes it a little more hassle, but much more attractive, than plain-old straight trim.

Cutting the Parts

1. Cut the following parts from redwood 1 x 8 and label each part with its identifying code.

Code	Length	Quantity
A	24 inches	4
B	16½ inches	2
C	8½ inches	2

2. The **A** pieces will serve as the front and back walls of the two boxes. Those for the upper box must be notched to fit over the end walls of the lower box. Cut a ¾ x ½-inch notch from two adjacent corners of one **A** piece, at the ends of one long edge (**Figure H**). Modify only one additional **A** piece in this manner, leaving two **A** pieces unaltered.

3. The **C** pieces will serve as the end walls of the upper box and must be trimmed to fit. Trim each **C** piece so that it measures 6¾ x 8½ inches.

4. Insert one of the spacer slats between each two trellis ribs flush at the top, as shown in **Figure F**. Glue the ends of the spacer slats to the ribs, and secure each joint with one or two staples.

5. Glue the upper slat along the top of the spacer-slat-and-rib assembly as shown in **Figure G**. Secure the upper slat with staples.

6. Now simply glue the heart sections in place, adjusting them up or down if necessary to achieve a good fit and proper alignment.

7. If you are going to plant the trellis, start digging. If you're going to build the planter box, read on.

BUILDING OUTDOOR FURNITURE

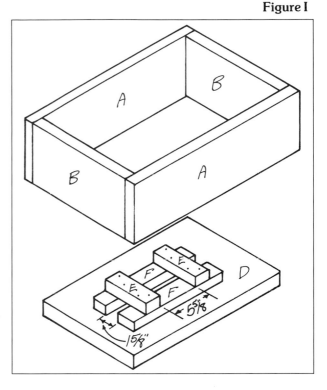

Figure I

4. Cut a 16½ x 22½-inch piece of ¾-inch wafer-wood or exterior plywood and label it D. This piece will serve as the planter floor. Drill five or six holes through the floor for drainage.

5. If you are not going to mount the trellis in the planter, skip this step and proceed to step 6. If you are going to mount the trellis in the planter, cut the pieces listed below from the specified scrap materials and label them as listed.

Code	Length	Quantity	Material
E	5¼ inches	2	1 x 2
F	12½ inches	2	2 x 2

6. Cut two 7 x 11-inch rectangles from ¼-inch wafer-wood or plywood and label each one G. These will serve to connect the upper and lower boxes.

7. We cut the trim pieces from redwood 1 x 3. (If you don't like to bevel and miter, stop right here and create your own trim design. We must have been bitten by the bevel bug the day we designed this trim, but you woodworkers know how that goes — sometimes you just get carried away.) To reproduce our trim, begin by setting your table saw to a 45-degree angle. Set the fence to a width of 2 inches. Run all of the 1 x 3 stock lengthwise through the saw to produce 2-inch-wide stock with one long edge beveled at 45 degrees.

8. You now have the basic stock from which to cut the trim pieces. As you can see in the assembly diagram, **Figure K**, the trim pieces are mitered to fit together at the corners. But because they are attached to the box walls at an angle, the end cuts must be compound miters, not simple miters. We found a very simple way of making these cuts, using a chop saw (power miter box). Set the chop saw to a 45-degree angle toward the right as you face the saw. Place one of the beveled 1 x 3s on the saw table, not flat but rather ON ITS BEVELED EDGE. It will be leaning away from the saw, because the beveled edge should be flat against the saw table. Pull the saw across the piece near the right-hand end to make the first compound miter. Now reset the saw to a 45-degree angle toward the left. Measure along the beveled edge 24 inches from the mitered corner and mark this point. Place the stock back on the saw table as you did before, on the beveled edge, ad-

justing it so that the blade will begin cutting at the marked point on the beveled edge. Make the cut, and that's it for the first trim piece. Cut three identical trim pieces and label each one H.

9. Use the same technique to cut two trim pieces that each measure 10 inches along the beveled edge. Label each one J.

10. The final four trim pieces are short ones and are each mitered on one end only. To create one of these pieces, begin by cutting across the stock as you did before, with the saw set toward the right. Measure along the beveled edge 3¼ inches and mark the point. Reset the saw and make a straight cut across the stock at the marked point. Label this piece I. For the second piece, measure from the straight-cut end 3¼ inches along the beveled edge and mark the point. Reset the saw to a 45-degree angle toward the left and cut across the stock at the marked point. This is the second I piece. Repeat this entire procedure to create two more I pieces, one cut toward the right and one cut toward the left. You now have all the trim pieces cut.

Assembly

1. The lower box and floor assembly, with the trellis support in place, is shown in **Figure I**. Use the two un-notched A pieces as the front and back walls, and the two B pieces as the end walls. Glue the four walls together, placing the end walls between the front and back walls, flush at the top and bottom, as shown. Secure the joints with finishing nails.

2. If you are going to mount the trellis in the planter, use the E and F pieces to build a support as shown in **Figure I**. Glue the two F pieces to the waferwood floor D, centering them lengthwise along the floor and allowing 1⅝ inches between them. Secure them with nails driven up through the bottom of the floor. Center the two E pieces crosswise on top of the F pieces, allowing 5⅝ inches between them. Glue and nail them securely to the F pieces.

3. Place the assembled walls over the floor (the floor will fit inside the walls), and secure with nails.

4. Now assemble the upper box walls. To do this, first glue the notched A front and back walls to the trimmed C end walls so that the A pieces cover the ends of the C pieces. All pieces should be flush at the top. The end walls should not extend down below the notches in the front and back walls. If they do, you have them turned the wrong way; the end walls are wider than they are tall. Secure the joints with finishing nails.

5. Place the upper box on top of the lower box as shown in **Figure J**. The upper end walls should rest flush on the lower ones, centered between the lower front and back walls. Glue the joints. Secure the boxes by driving finishing nails through the lower end walls into the notched edges of the upper front and back walls. Use the two thin waferwood G pieces as connectors on the insides on the upper and lower end walls. Glue them in place and secure with staples.

6. Figure K shows the planter with the trim attached. The H pieces serve as trim for the front and back walls on both tiers. The I pieces serve as trim for the lower end walls, and the J pieces serve as trim for the upper end walls. Each trim piece is glued, beveled edge down, along the upper edge of the wall. You may need to use a rasp or file to get a perfect fit at all corners. Secure the trim pieces with finishing nails.

Figure J

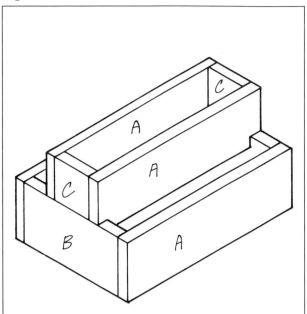

Figure K

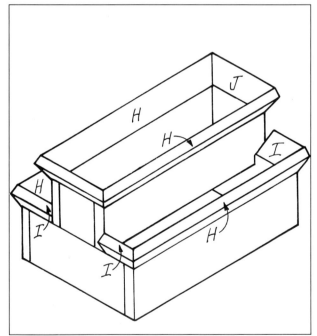

7. Lower the end of the trellis into the support structure, and you've got a planter/trellis to love.

Garden Planter Bench

Here's a durable and beautiful garden bench that will keep you sittin' pretty. Each section is 6 feet long, 17 inches wide, and 19 inches high. It's incredibly easy to build. Once you have the basic idea you'll probably want to create custom benches for all your favorite garden settings (or sittings).

Materials

Note: The corner bench that we made consists of two sections joined at right angles. If your garden or patio will not accommodate a corner bench, you may prefer to make one or more single straight benches and forgo the corner model. For this reason, we have listed separately the materials required to build the corner bench shown here and a single straight bench that will stand on its own.

Lattice: The latticework on the planter boxes is made from ¼ x 1½-inch redwood strips ripped from larger stock. One 2 x 4 redwood board, 8 feet long, will provide enough lattice to complete all the required work on one planter box. For each corner bench you make, you'll need enough lattice to cover three planter boxes. A single straight bench requires enough lattice to cover two planter boxes.

In addition to the redwood for the lattice, you'll need the following amounts of lumber.

For the corner bench:

86 linear feet of 2 x 4 redwood

15 linear feet of 2 x 2 redwood

18 linear feet of 1 x 3 redwood (Note: The 1 x 3 redwood must be planed to ⅝ inch thick. You can accomplish this using a table saw, or you can have the boards planed at the lumberyard.)

One 4 x 8-foot sheet of ¾-inch waferwood or exterior-grade plywood

Eight No. 12 gauge flathead Phillips wood screws, each 2¼ inches long

4d and 16d common nails

For the straight bench:

47 linear feet of 2 x 4 redwood

10 linear feet of 2 x 2 redwood

12 linear feet of 1 x 3 redwood (see note above)

3 x 8-foot piece of ¾-inch waferwood or exterior-grade plywood

4d and 16d common nails

Whichever bench design you choose to build, you'll be constructing the planter boxes first and then adding the slat-style seat structures. Each planter consists of a

Figure A

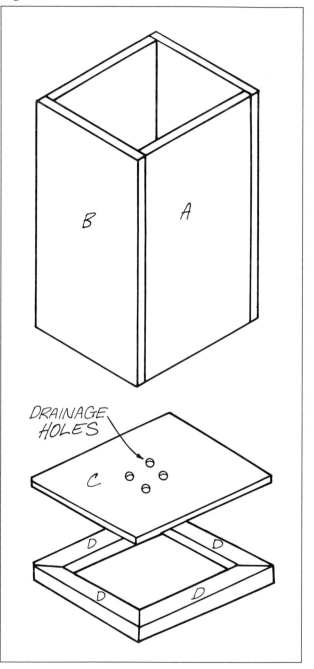

basic waferwood or plywood box covered with latticework. Begin by ripping one 8-foot redwood 2 x 4 into lattice strips for each planter box.

Building the Planter Boxes

1. Dimensions of the planter box walls and floor are listed below. Cut the parts from waferwood or plywood and label each with its identifying code. Quantities specified are for one planter box.

Code	Dimensions	Quantity
A	12 x 16 inches	2
B	13½ x 16 inches	2
C	12 x 12 inches	1

2. Additional parts required for the planter box are listed below. Cut the parts from the specified materials and label each with its code.

Code	Length	Quantity	Material
D	11½ inches	4	2 x 4
E	13½ inches	8	lattice

3. Nail together the four box walls (**A** and **B** pieces), butting the edges as shown in **Figure A**.

4. The **C** piece serves as the floor. For drainage, drill three or four holes through the **C** piece, near the center. Lower the box over the **C** piece until it is flush with the bottom, and nail it in place.

5. The **D** pieces are used to build a base for the planter box. Miter both ends of each **D** piece at a 45-degree angle and nail the base together (**Figure A**). Center the base under the box floor and nail it in place.

6. Draw a line around the planter box, 3½ inches below the upper edge. This line designates the upper limit of the latticework. Begin assembling the latticework on one side of the box at the lower left-hand corner, and work diagonally upward. Miter the ends of one lattice strip to fit close to the corner, at a 45-degree angle to the edge of the wall (**Figure B**). Tack the strip in place and then miter and add a second strip, allowing a 1½-inch space between them. An easy way to achieve even spacing is to use a spare lattice strip as a spacer. Continue adding strips until you reach the opposite upper corner (formed by the pencil line and the right-hand edge of the box). This completes the first latticework layer.

7. Repeat the procedures in step 6 to create a second latticework layer on top of the first one, beginning at the

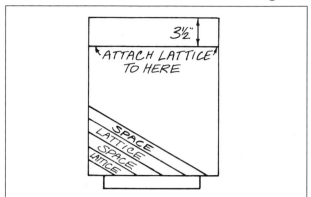

Figure C

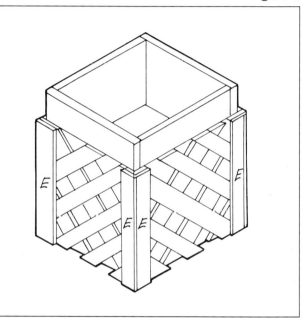

lower right-hand corner and working upward. The strips of the second layer should be perpendicular to those of the first layer.

8. Repeat the procedures in steps 6 and 7 to cover each of the remaining box walls with latticework.

9. Nail the **E** pieces along the sides of the latticework on each wall, as shown in **Figure C**. The planter box is now complete.

10. Build one identical planter box for the straight bench design. Build two additional boxes if you're constructing a corner bench.

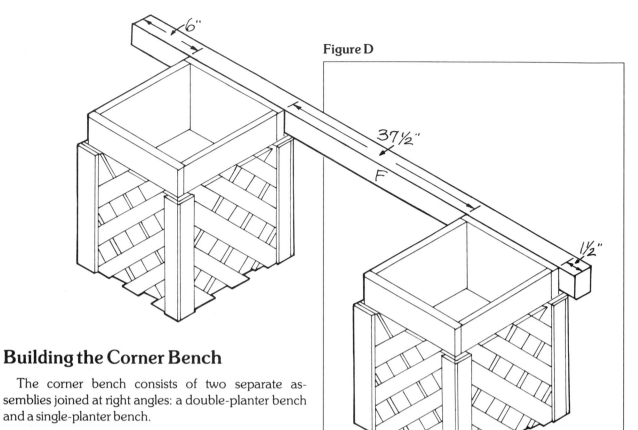

Figure D

Building the Corner Bench

The corner bench consists of two separate assemblies joined at right angles: a double-planter bench and a single-planter bench.

1. Cut the parts listed below from the specified materials, and label each with its identifying code.

Code	Length	Quantity	Material
F	72 inches	2	2 x 4
G	70½ inches	1	2 x 4
H	57 inches	1	2 x 4
I	6 inches	12	2 x 4
J	37½ inches	12	2 x 4
K	3½ inches	56	1 x 3 (planed)

2. To build the double-planter section of the corner bench, align two assembled planter boxes 37½ inches apart. Place an F piece along one side of the boxes, with one wide side of the board against the boxes, between the top of the latticework and the upper box edges. Adjust the F piece so that it extends 6 inches beyond one box and 1½ inches beyond the other (**Figure D**). Nail the F piece in place from inside the boxes.

3. The thinner K pieces serve as spacers between the 2 x 4 seat slats, as shown in **Figures E**, **F**, and **G**. Refer to **Figure E** as you nail one K spacer to the attached

F slat at each of the following locations: one on each side of the left-hand planter box, one at the midpoint between the two boxes, and one on the inner side of the right-hand box. All of the spacers should be flush with the upper and lower edges of the F slat.

4. On the outer side of the left-hand box, nail an I slat to the spacer as shown in **Figure F**. In addition, nail a J slat to the three spacers between the two boxes (**Figure F**). The upper and lower edges of all pieces should be even.

5. Continue adding K spacers and J and I slats in this manner until you reach the opposite side of the planter boxes. The last row you add should be a row of K spacers. To complete the assembly, place the G slat along the front side of the boxes as shown in **Figure G**. The slat should extend 6 inches beyond the left-hand box

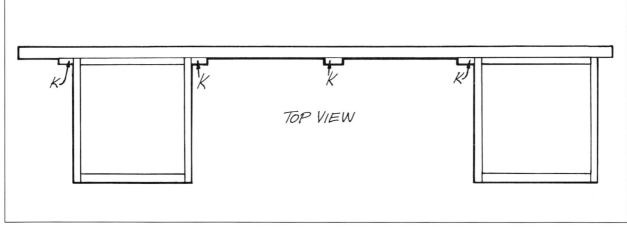

TOP VIEW

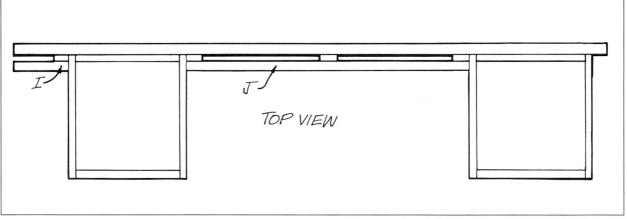

TOP VIEW

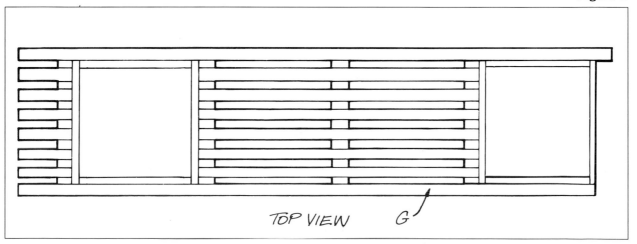

TOP VIEW

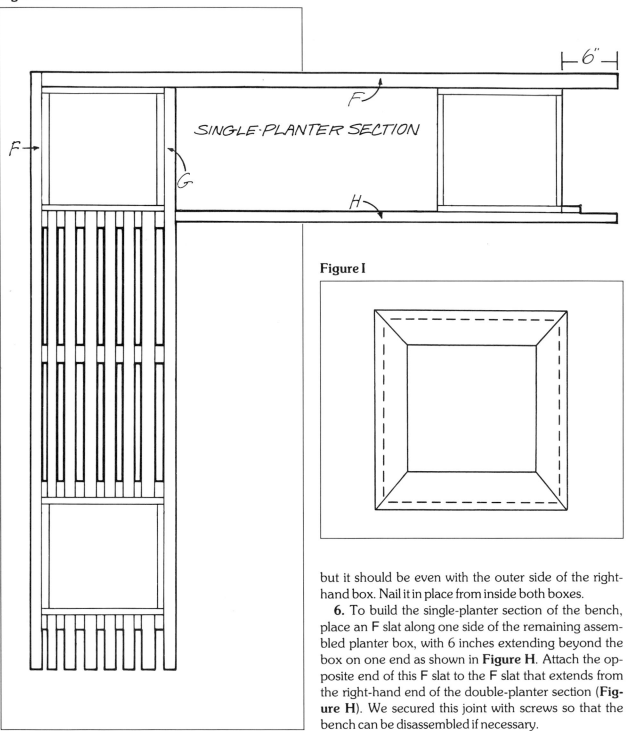

SINGLE-PLANTER SECTION

Figure I

but it should be even with the outer side of the right-hand box. Nail it in place from inside both boxes.

6. To build the single-planter section of the bench, place an F slat along one side of the remaining assembled planter box, with 6 inches extending beyond the box on one end as shown in **Figure H**. Attach the opposite end of this F slat to the F slat that extends from the right-hand end of the double-planter section (**Figure H**). We secured this joint with screws so that the bench can be disassembled if necessary.

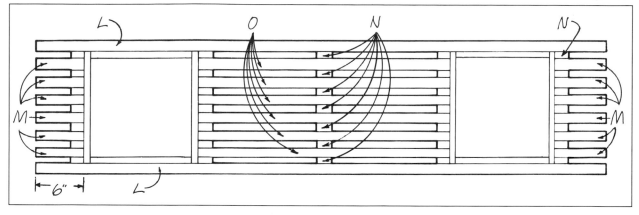

7. Build the seat using K spacers and J and I slats in the same manner as you did the double-planter seat. Nail the H slat to the opposite side of the planter box, butting one end against the G slat of the double-planter section as shown in **Figure H**. Insert screws from inside the corner planter box into the ends of the I slats of the single-planter section.

8. Each planter box has a top frame that extends above the seat. Cut four 13½-inch lengths of 2 x 2 and miter both ends of each length at a 45-degree angle. Nail the four lengths to the top of one planter box, forming a frame as shown in **Figure I**.

9. Cut and miter four additional lengths of 2 x 2 for each of the other planter boxes, and attach them in the same manner.

Building a Straight Bench

The straight stand-alone bench is similar to the double-planter section of the corner bench. You can alter the length and/or depth quite easily, now that you know how it all goes together. This straight bench is 6 feet long, 16½ inches deep, and 19 inches tall.

1. Cut the parts listed below from the specified materials and label each with its identifying code.

Code	Length	Quantity	Material
L	72 inches	2	2 x 4
M	6 inches	12	2 x 4
N	3½ inches	35	1 x 3 (planed)
O	33 inches	6	2 x 4

2. A top view of the assembled bench is shown in **Figure J**. To begin, align two assembled planter boxes 33 inches apart. Place one L slat along one side of the boxes, with one wide side of the slat against the boxes, between the top of the latticework and the upper box edges. Adjust the slat so that it extends evenly 6 inches beyond each box as shown. Nail the slat in place from inside each box.

3. Nail an N spacer to the L slat on each side of each planter box, and at the midpoint between the two boxes (**Figure J**). All the spacers should be even with the upper and lower edges of the L slat.

4. On the outer side of each box, nail an M slat to the spacer, as shown in **Figure J**. Nail an O slat to the three spacers between the two boxes. The upper and lower edges of all pieces should be even.

5. Continue adding N spacers and M and O slats in this manner until you reach the opposite sides of the planter boxes. To complete the assembly, place the remaining L slat along the front side of the boxes, aligning the ends with those of the other slats, and nail from inside both boxes.

6. Each planter box has a top frame that extends above the seat. Cut four 13½-inch lengths from the 2 x 2, and miter both ends of each length at a 45-degree angle. Nail the four lengths of 2 x 2 to the top of one planter box, as shown in **Figure I**.

7. Cut and miter four additional lengths of 2 x 2 for the second planter box, and attach them to the top of that box in the same manner.

Redwood Gazebo Bench

This latticework bench balances just the right amounts of openness, privacy, airiness, and shade. It measures 6½ feet long, providing space for four adults, 6 feet tall, and 2 feet deep.

Materials

The lattice is made by ripping ¼ x 1½-inch redwood strips from larger stock. Five 2 x 6 redwood boards, each 10 feet long, will provide enough lattice to complete all of the required work.

In addition to the redwood lumber for the lattice, you'll need the following amounts of stock for the bench:

80 linear feet of 2 x 4 redwood

7 linear feet of 2 x 6 redwood

130 linear feet of ¾ x ¾-inch redwood stripping

For the solid parts, we used ⁷⁄₁₆-inch waferwood, but ½-inch exterior grade plywood will work just as well. All the parts can be cut from a 4 x 6-foot piece.

Galvanized 8d and 2d common nails

Galvanized tacks

The bench consists of five sections: two identical side sections, a back section that is identical to the sides except in length, the seat and connecting pieces, and the finish trim. We suggest that you begin by ripping the five 2 x 6 redwood boards into lattice strips so you won't have to interrupt your work to cut them.

Building the Side Sections

Each side of the bench consists of an outer frame made of 2 x 4s, with a latticework insert in the upper portion and a waferwood insert in the center portion. The inserts are held in place by support frames made of redwood stripping. An exploded view of one complete side section is provided in **Figure A** and an assembled view is shown in **Figure D**.

1. The parts required to build the two side sections are listed below. Cut the parts and label each with its identifying code.

Code	Length	Quantity	Material
Outer frames:			
A	72 inches	4	2 x 4
B	21 inches	6	2 x 4
Support frames:			
C	40½ inches	8	¾ x ¾
D	10 inches	8	¾ x ¾
E	21 inches	16	¾ x ¾

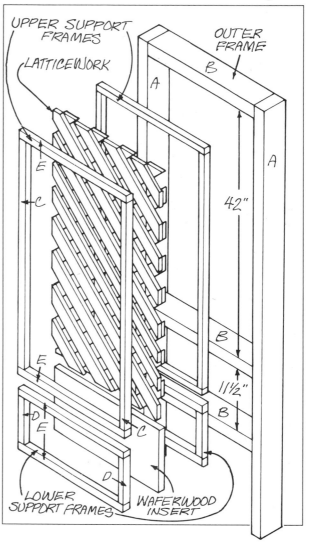

Figure A

2. In addition, cut two waferwood inserts, each 11½ x 21 inches.

3. To make the outer frame for one side section, glue and nail together two A and three B pieces, butting the ends as shown in **Figure A**. Allow 42 inches between the upper and middle B pieces, and 11½ inches between the middle and lower B pieces.

4. The next step is to assemble one of the support frames inside the outer frame you just built. As shown in **Figure A**, the upper section of the support frame consists of two horizontal E pieces and two vertical C

Figure B

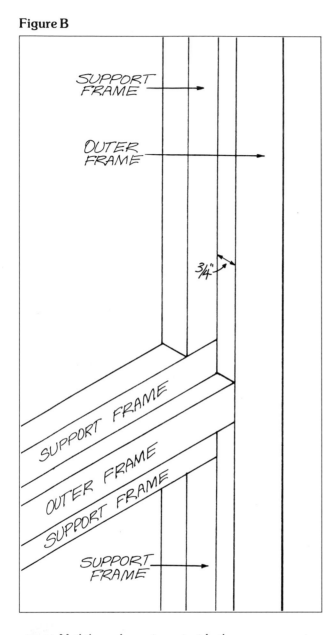

SUPPORT FRAME

OUTER FRAME

3/4"

SUPPORT FRAME

OUTER FRAME

SUPPORT FRAME

SUPPORT FRAME

Figure C

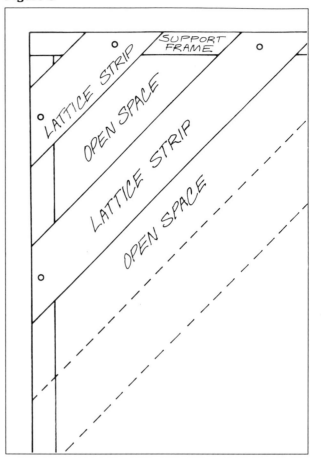

LATTICE STRIP

SUPPORT FRAME

OPEN SPACE

LATTICE STRIP

OPEN SPACE

pieces. Nail these four pieces inside the upper opening of the frame you built in step 3, butting the ends as shown and placing the support frame ¾ inch from one side of the outer frame (**Figure B**). The lower section of the support frame consists of two horizontal E pieces and two vertical D pieces. Nail these four pieces inside the center opening of the outer frame, ¾ inch from the same side.

5. Begin assembling the latticework inside the upper portion of the frame, as shown in **Figure C**. Miter the ends of one lattice strip to fit close to the upper left-hand corner, at a 45-degree angle to the horizontal and vertical pieces of the support frame, and tack it in place. Miter and add a second lattice strip, allowing a 1½-inch space between the first and second strips. An easy way to achieve even spacing is to use an extra lattice strip as a spacer. Continue mitering and adding lattice strips in this manner until you reach the lower right-hand corner. This completes the first lattice layer.

6. Repeat the procedures in step 5 to create a second lattice layer on top of the first one. This time, begin in the lower left-hand corner and work to the upper right-hand corner, so that the strips of the second layer are at a 90-degree angle to those of the first layer.

Figure D

Figure E

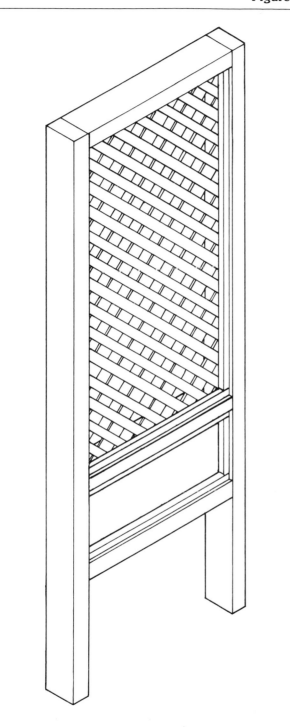

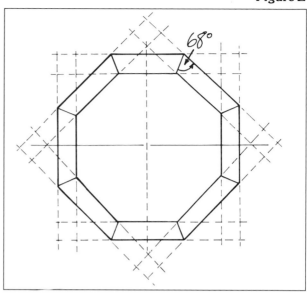

7. When you have completed the latticework, nail the E and C pieces of the second support frame in place, flush against the latticework and the outer frame. The latticework should be sandwiched between the two support frames.

8. Place one of the waferwood inserts inside the center opening of the frame, flush against the support frame. Nail the E and D pieces of the second support frame in place, flush against the waferwood and the outer frame. The waferwood should be sandwiched between the two support frames, and the completed side section should now look like the one shown in **Figure D**.

9. Repeat the procedures in steps 3 through 8 to build a second, identical side section.

Octagonal Windows

If you wish, you can create an octagonal window in one or both side sections. It is not difficult to do and provides an attractive design feature. To make a window, you simply attach a frame to each side of the latticework and then cut out the lattice strips inside the frame.

1. For each window you wish to make cut sixteen 5½-inch lengths from lattice. Cut both ends of each piece at a 22-degree angle (**Figure E**).

Figure F

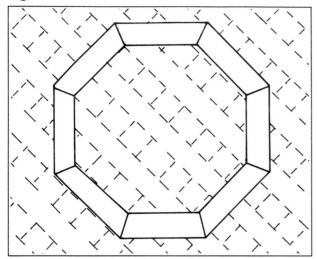

Figure G

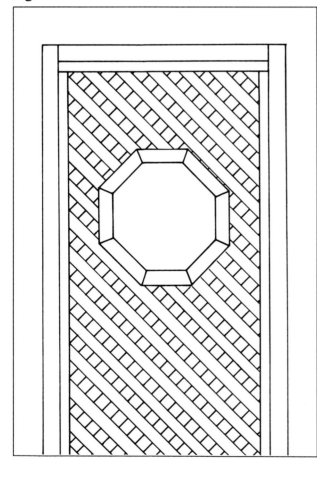

2. Combine eight strips to form an octagon (**Figure F**). On one bench side section, place the octagon on one side of the latticework, 5½ inches from the top horizontal piece of the outer frame and centered between the sides. Tack the octagon in place. Use another eight strips to create a second octagon on the opposite side of the latticework, matching the position of the first octagon. Tack the second octagon in place.

3. Use a saber saw to cut the latticework from the center of the octagonal frame, as shown in **Figure G**.

4. Repeat the procedures in this section to create a window in the remaining side section.

Building the Back Section

The back section is identical to the side sections except that it is quite a bit longer. It consists of an outer frame, latticework and waferwood inserts, and support frames that hold them in place.

1. The parts required to build the back section are listed below. Cut the parts and label each with its identifying code.

Code	Length	Quantity	Material
Outer frame:			
F	72 inches	2	2 x 4
G	62 inches	3	2 x 4
Support frames:			
H	40½ inches	4	¾ x ¾
I	10 inches	4	¾ x ¾
J	62 inches	8	¾ x ¾

2. Cut an 11½ x 62-inch waferwood insert.

3. The back section is assembled in the same manner as the side sections were. Begin by building the outer frame, using the F pieces as verticals and the G pieces as horizontals, butting the pieces as shown in **Figure H**. Allow 42 inches between the upper and middle horizontals, and 11½ inches between the middle and lower horizontals.

4. Next, install a support frame inside the upper opening and another inside the middle opening, ¾ inch from one side of the outer frame. As indicated in

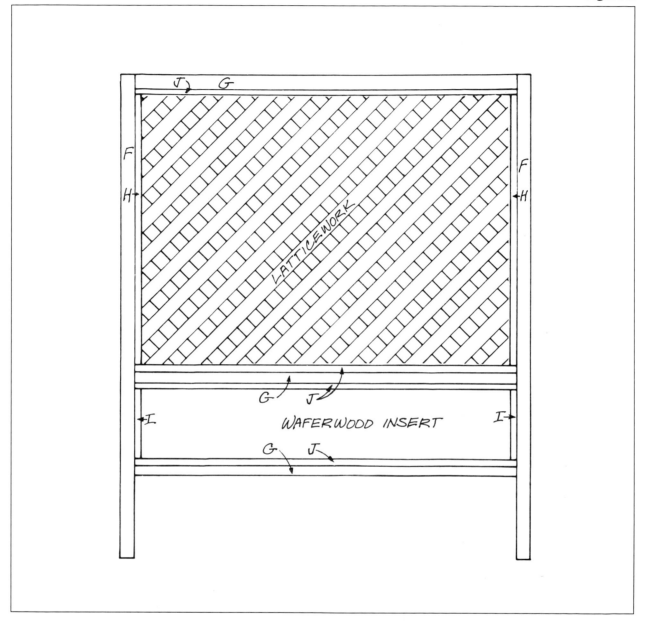

Figure G, use H and J pieces for the support frame in the upper opening, and use I and J pieces for the middle opening. Butt the ends of the support-frame pieces as shown.

5. Assemble the first layer of latticework, nailing the ends of the strips to the support-frame pieces, and then work in the opposite direction to add the second layer. Secure the latticework by installing the second support frame in the upper opening.

6. Install the waferwood insert, nail it to the support-frame pieces, and then add the second support frame in the middle opening.

Figure I

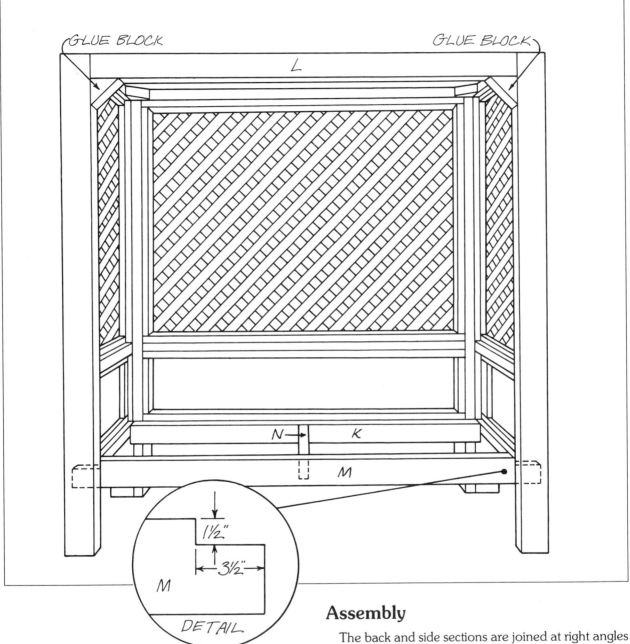

Assembly

The back and side sections are joined at right angles with horizontal braces at the upper and lower stress points. The seat rests on the lower braces. The assembly is shown in **Figure I**.

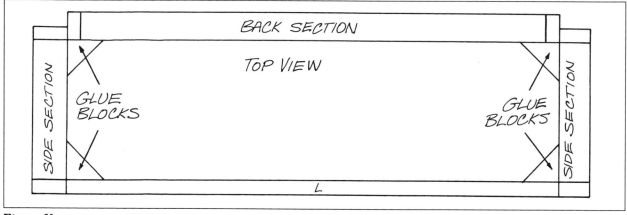

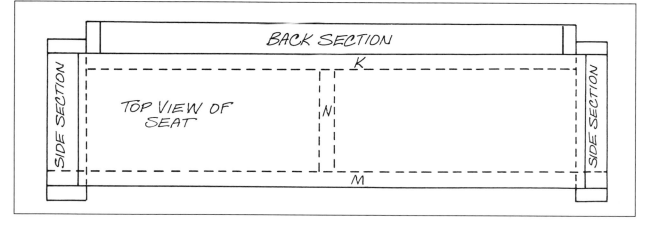

1. The additional parts required to brace the bench are listed below. Cut the parts and label each with its identifying code.

Code	Length	Quantity	Material
K	65 inches	1	2 x 4
L	65 inches	1	2 x 4
M	72 inches	1	2 x 6
N	18 inches	1	2 x 4
O	3½ inches	3	2 x 4

2. Cut one seat from waferwood, 66½ x 21 inches.

3. First, nail the K piece to the back section as shown in **Figure I**, flush with the tops of the side-section B pieces and the back-section G piece.

4. Cut each of the three O pieces in half along the diagonal to form six triangular glue blocks.

5. Align the three bench sections as shown in **Figure I**. Install the top brace (the L piece) between the two side sections at the front, securing it with a glue block at each corner as shown. Use the remaining four glue blocks to secure each upper corner of the bench assembly, as shown in the top view illustration, **Figure J**.

6. The M piece serves as the lower front brace, and is notched to fit underneath the lower B piece of each side section. Cut a notch at each end of the M piece, referring to the magnified detail drawing in **Figure I**, and install the brace as shown.

7. The N piece serves as a center brace. Nail it to the M and K pieces as shown in **Figure I**.

8. Figure K shows a top view of the waferwood seat in place inside the bench. The dotted lines indicate the

Figure L

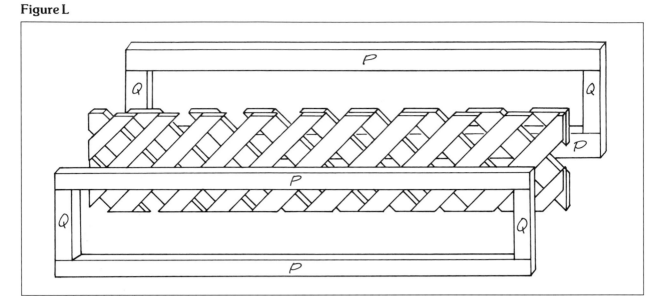

Figure M

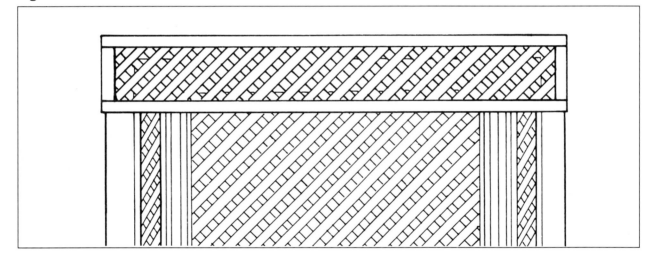

pieces on which the seat rests: the **K** piece at the back, the **M** piece at the front, the **N** piece across the center, and a portion of the lower **B** piece of each side section. Place the waferwood seat on top of the braces and nail it in place along the front, back, sides, and center.

Adding the Trim

The gazebo bench has a front trim assembly consisting of framed latticework (**Figures L** and **M**), and a latticework roof.

1. For the front trim assembly, cut the frame pieces listed below from lattice strips.

Code	Length	Quantity
P	72 inches	4
Q	5 inches	4

2. Use two **P** and two **Q** pieces to assemble one frame, butting them as shown in **Figure L**. Make a second frame in the same manner.

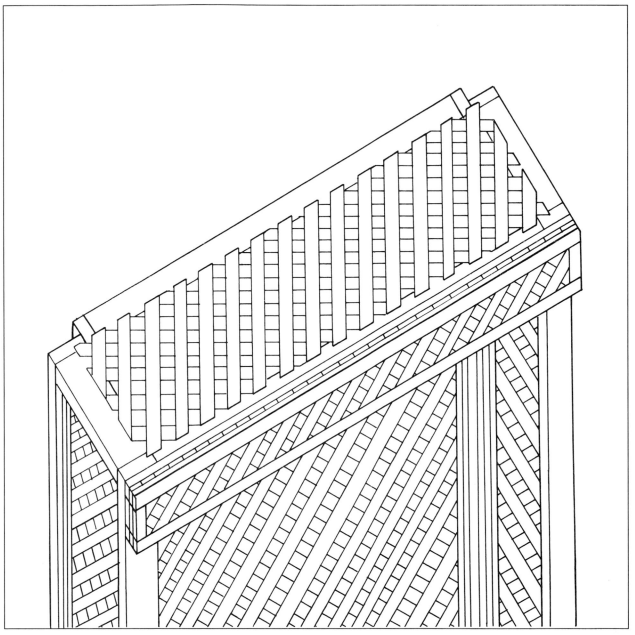

3. Place one of the frames on a flat surface and construct the latticework in two layers as you did for the side and back sections. Nail the remaining frame over the completed latticework.

4. Nail the completed front trim assembly to the front of the gazebo bench, flush with the top and with both sides (**Figure M**).

5. Construct a latticework roof as shown in **Figure N** by cutting and nailing two layers of lattice strips to the bench top. No frame is required.

Planter Table

This attractive patio or lawn table features a planter box covered with latticework, and is a perfect companion piece to the redwood gazebo bench. The tabletop measures roughly 34 x 48 inches, and stands 16 inches high. The planter box is 12 inches square.

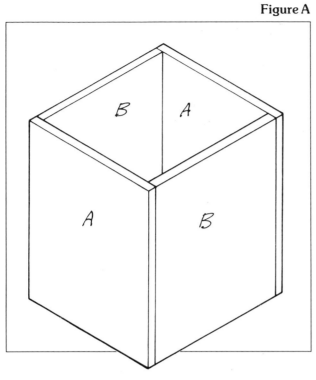

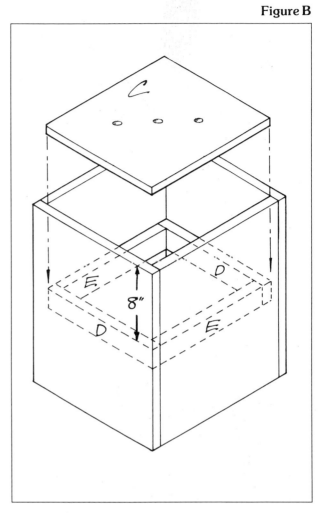

Materials

The lattice is made by ripping ¼ x 1½-inch redwood
strips from larger stock. One 2 x 4 redwood board,
8 feet long, will provide enough lattice to complete
all of the required work.

In addition to the redwood for the lattice, you'll need
the following amounts of lumber:

9 linear feet of 1 x 2 redwood
6 linear feet of 2 x 2 redwood
45 linear feet of 2 x 4 redwood
4 linear feet of 2 x 6 redwood

We used ⁷⁄₁₆-inch waferwood for the planter box base,
but you may wish to substitute ½-inch exterior
grade plywood. The required parts can be cut from
a 33 x 36-inch piece.

Galvanized 2d and 8d common nails
Galvanized tacks

The table is made in two sections: the waferwood-
and-latticework planter box, and the tabletop with sup-
porting structures. Begin by ripping the 8-foot redwood
2 x 4 into lattice strips.

Building the Planter Box

The planter box is quite simple to make. The four
walls are assembled using butt joints, and the floor rests
on supports above ground level. The latticework is
added after the box is assembled.

1. Dimensions of the planter box walls and floor are
listed below. Cut the parts from waferwood or plywood
and label each with its identifying code.

Code	Dimensions	Quantity
A	12½ x 16 inches	2
B	11½ x 16 inches	2
C	11½ x 11½ inches	1

Figure C

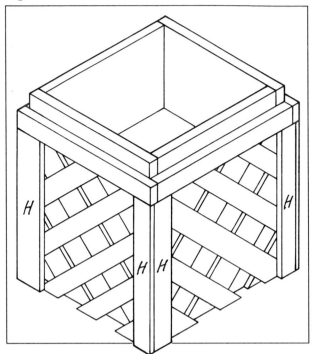

Figure D

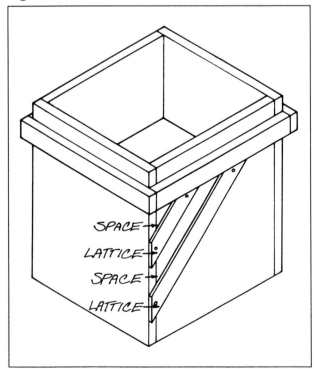

Figure E

2. Additional parts required for the planter box are listed below. Cut the parts from the specified materials and label each with its code.

Code	Length	Quantity	Material
D	11½ inches	2	1 x 2
E	10 inches	2	1 x 2
F	14 inches	2	1 x 2
G	12½ inches	2	1 x 2
H	13 inches	8	lattice

3. Nail together the four box walls (**A** and **B** pieces), butting the edges as shown in **Figure A**.

4. The D and E pieces serve as supports for the floor. Nail them inside the box walls as shown in **Figure B**, about 8 inches down from the top.

5. Drill three or four ½-inch-diameter holes through the C piece, for drainage, and then lower it into the box so that it rests on the supports. Nail it in place.

6. The F and G pieces serve as supports for the tabletop. Nail them to the outside of the box, 1½ inches down from the top (**Figure C**).

BUILDING OUTDOOR FURNITURE

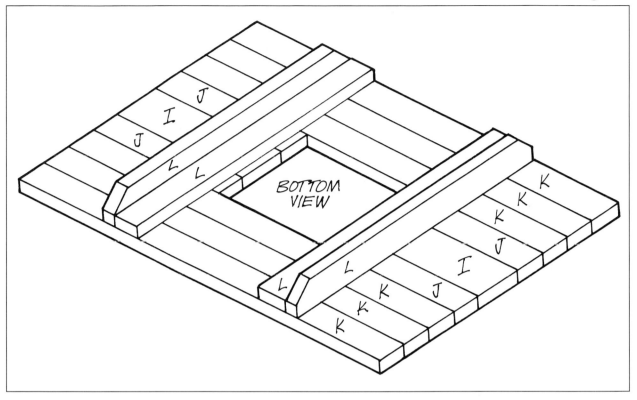

7. Begin assembling the latticework on one side of the box, below the tabletop support. Miter the ends of one lattice strip to fit close to the upper left-hand corner, at a 45-degree angle to the edges of the wall and tabletop support (**Figure D**). Tack the strip in place and then miter and add a second strip, allowing a 1½-inch space between them. Continue mitering and adding strips until you reach the opposite lower corner. This completes the first latticework layer.

8. Repeat the procedures in step 7 to create a second latticework layer on top of the first one, beginning at the lower left-hand corner and working upward. The strips of the second layer should be at a 90-degree angle to those of the first layer.

9. Repeat the procedures in steps 7 and 8 to cover each of the remaining box walls with latticework.

10. Nail the H pieces along the sides of the latticework on each wall as shown in **Figure E**. The planter box is now complete.

Building the Tabletop

The tabletop consists of redwood boards connected by braces. An opening in the center allows the tabletop to rest on the planter box supports.

1. The parts required for the tabletop are listed below. Cut the parts from the specified materials and label each with its identifying code.

Code	Length	Quantity	Material
I	17½ inches	2	2 x 6
J	17½ inches	4	2 x 4
K	47½ inches	6	2 x 4
L	33½ inches	4	2 x 4
M	3½ inches	2	2 x 4

2. The I, J, and K pieces serve as the tabletop slats, and the L and M pieces serve as supports. Arrange the I, J, and K slats on a flat work surface as shown in **Figure F**, leaving a center opening 12½ inches square. If

Figure G

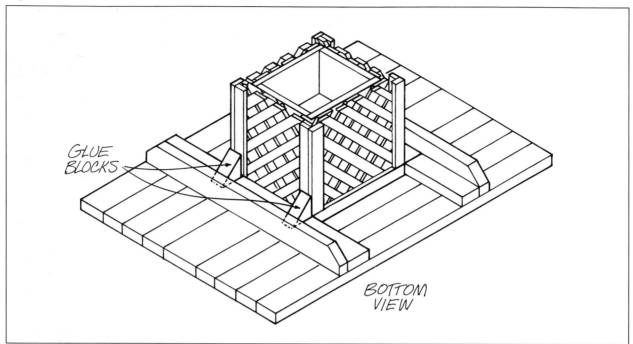

GLUE
BLOCKS

BOTTOM
VIEW

Figure H

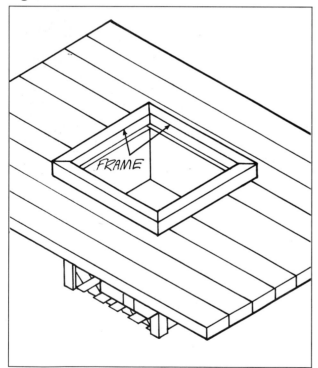

FRAME

any of the slats are better looking on one side than on the other, turn the good side down, as you will be working on the underside of the tabletop. Place one L support across the slats, wide side down, ⅞ inch from one edge of the opening. Nail it in place. Attach a second L support to the slats ⅞ inch from the opposite edge of the opening.

3. Trim two corners of each remaining L support, as shown in **Figure F**. Place the trimmed supports across the slats as shown, long edge down, and nail them to the first two L supports.

4. Cut each of the M pieces in half along the diagonal to form four triangular glue blocks. Place the assembled tabletop over the planter box and nail the glue blocks to the flat L supports and to the sides of the box as shown in **Figure G**.

Final Assembly

1. Cut four 15½-inch lengths of redwood 2 x 2, and miter both ends of each length at a 45-degree angle.

2. Nail the four lengths of 2 x 2 to the top of the planter box as a frame (**Figure H**).

BUILDING OUTDOOR FURNITURE

Yard Swing

Catch the evening breezes in this roomy, easy-to-build yard swing. It's made entirely of redwood 2 x 2s and 1-inch dowel rods, and will take a standard patio chair cushion. Your swinging leisure hours will be vastly improved by the yard swing as it's shown here, but you might wish to be more expansive and make a double-wide! Overall dimensions of the swing are roughly 27 x 31 x 24 inches.

Figure A

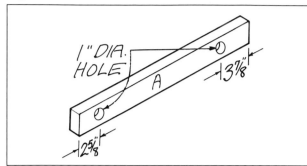

Figure B

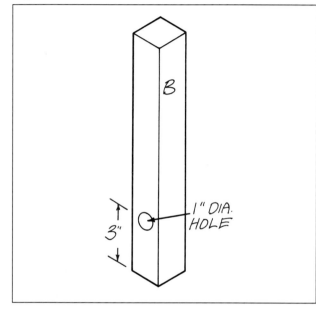

Materials

24 linear feet of 2 x 2 redwood

1 linear foot of 2 x 4 redwood

40 feet of 1-inch wooden dowel rod

1 foot of ⅜-inch wooden dowel rod

Fifty-four No. 6 gauge flathead wood screws, each 1 inch long

Eight 6d common nails

Rope: We used approximately 15 yards of 1,000-pound-test nylon ski rope to hang the swing.

Cushion: A standard patio chair cushion, 22 to 28 inches wide, 40 to 46 inches long, and as thick as you like, will fit the swing.

The yard swing consists of four separate sections: the seat, the back, and two identical side sections. The side sections are simple rectangles made of 2 x 2s. The seat and back sections are quite similar to one another, each being composed of two 2 x 2 side members joined by lengths of dowel.

Cutting the Parts

1. Cut the parts listed below from redwood 2 x 2 and label each with its identifying code.

Code	Length	Quantity
A	28 inches	4
B	15 inches	6
C	27 inches	2

2. Corner glue blocks are used to reinforce the side sections. Cut two 3½-inch lengths of redwood 2 x 4. Cut each one in half along the diagonal so that you have four triangular blocks. Label each block D.

3. Cut the parts listed below from 1-inch dowel rod and label each with its identifying code.

Code	Length	Quantity
E	23¼ inches	13
F	26¼ inches	1
G	31½ inches	3
H	4 inches	2

4. Cut four 2½-inch lengths of ⅜-inch dowel rod and label each piece I. These will be used as holding pegs for the rope.

5. The A pieces will serve as the upper and lower members of the two side sections and must be drilled to accommodate two dowels each. A cutting diagram is provided in **Figure A**. As you work, drill the holes in as straight a line as possible or you're going to be deeply repentant when it's time to assemble the swing. As shown in **Figure A**, drill a 1-inch-diameter hole through one A piece, placing the center of the hole 3⅞ inches from one end. This will be the back of the A piece. Drill a second 1-inch-diameter hole through the same A piece along the same axis, placing the center of this hole 2⅝ inches from the opposite end. This will be the front end. It's important that the holes in the four A pieces

Figure C

be perfectly aligned, so use the **A** piece that you have already drilled as a guide to drill two holes in each of the remaining **A** pieces. It's a good idea to mark the ends as "front" and "back," to prevent confusion in the assembly process.

6. Two of the **B** pieces will serve as the front uprights in the two side sections and must be drilled to accommodate one dowel each. A cutting diagram is provided in **Figure B**. As with the **A** pieces, drill in as straight a line as possible. (That goes for all the drilling in this project.) Drill a 1-inch-diameter hole through one **B** piece, placing the center of the hole 3 inches from one end. This will be the lower end. Use the drilled **B** piece as a guide to drill one of the other **B** pieces only.

7. Two of the remaining **B** pieces will serve as the side members of the back section and must be drilled to accommodate the back-slat dowels. A cutting diagram is provided in **Figure C**. Drill five 1-inch-diameter holes through one **B** piece, each along the same axis as shown. Place the center of the first hole 2½ inches from one end, and place the centers of the succeeding holes at 2½-inch intervals. The center hole will house a longer dowel that serves to connect the back section to the side sections. If you enlarge this hole slightly, you will be able to pivot the back section to various angles for adjustable seating comfort. Don't go overboard when enlarging the hole, though, or there won't be enough friction to hold the back section in the various positions. Use the drilled **B** piece as a guide to drill one additional **B** piece to serve as the other side member of the back section.

8. The **C** pieces will serve as the side members of the seat section and must be drilled to accommodate the seat-slat dowels. A cutting diagram is provided in **Figure D**. Drill eleven 1-inch-diameter holes through one **C** piece, each along the same axis as shown. The center of the first hole should be placed ¾ inch from what will be the front end. Place the centers of the succeeding holes at 2½-inch intervals, which should place the center of the last hole about 1¼ inches from the back end. Use the drilled **C** piece as a guide to drill the second **C** piece, and mark the designated ends of each **C** piece as "front" or "back."

9. The three **G** dowels will serve as the connecting rods that join the back and seat sections to the side sec-

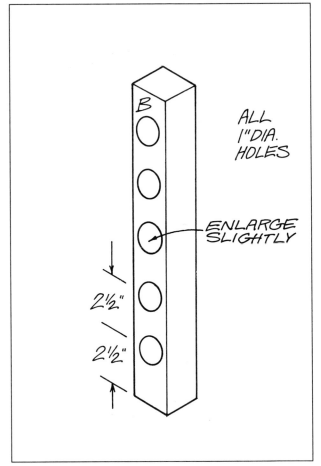

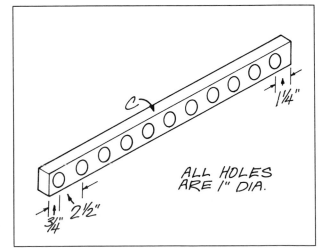

Figure D

Figure E

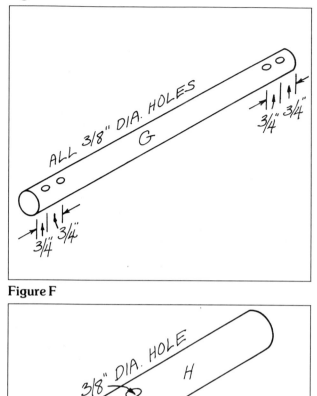

ALL 3/8" DIA. HOLES
G
3/4" 3/4"
3/4" 3/4"

Figure F

3/8" DIA. HOLE
H
1½"

tions. They extend out past the side sections and are drilled so that the rope may be passed through them and tied securely. Two of the G dowels are also drilled to accommodate holding pegs that help keep the tied rope from slipping off the ends. A cutting diagram is provided in **Figure E**. Drill four ⅜-inch-diameter holes through one of the G dowels, placing the center of the first hole ¾ inch from one end. Allow ¾ inch between the centers of the first and second holes. Repeat these drilling procedures near the opposite end of the same G dowel. Use the drilled G dowel as a guide to drill four holes in a second G dowel. For the third G dowel, drill only the two innermost holes. Do not drill the holes that are closest to the ends.

10. The short H dowels will serve as rope guides near the front of each side-section top member, where it is not possible to put a long connecting dowel. A cutting diagram is provided in **Figure F**. Drill a single ⅜-inch-diameter hole through one of the H dowels, 1½ inches from one end. This will be the outer end. Drill the second H dowel in the same manner, and mark the designated end of each as the "outer" end.

Building the Sections

1. An assembled side section is shown in **Figure G**. Glue together two A pieces and two B pieces, butting the ends as shown, and glue a triangular block D in each lower corner. Be sure to use a B piece that has no drilled holes as the back upright, and one that has only one drilled hole as the front upright, placing the hole near the lower end. In addition, be sure that the A pieces are turned the same way end for end, and that the ends designated as "front" are butted against the drilled B piece, not against the undrilled B piece. One last admonition, which should be pretty obvious, is to make certain the drilled pieces are rotated so that all holes run in the same direction. Secure each A-to-B joint using two screws, and secure each block D using two nails. Build a second identical side section.

2. The assembled back section is shown in **Figure H**. Use the remaining two B pieces, which should be the ones that have five holes each. If they're not, you either boo-boo'd in the cutting and drilling or you used one or both of these B pieces in the side sections. We'll let you figure out what went wrong. For those who indeed have the proper B pieces with which to work, congratulations. Place them about 20 inches apart, with the holes aligned, and insert the four E dowels into the two upper and two lower holes in each piece, leaving the center holes open. Adjust the spacing so that the ends of the dowels are flush with the outer edges of the B pieces, and glue the dowels in place. Secure each end of each dowel by inserting a screw through one side of the B piece, into the dowel. Insert all of the screws from the same side of the assembly, which will be the back side. Countersink the screws and, if you like, fill the recesses with wood filler or wooden plugs.

3. For the center dowel of the back section, use the G dowel that has only two drilled holes as shown in **Fig-**

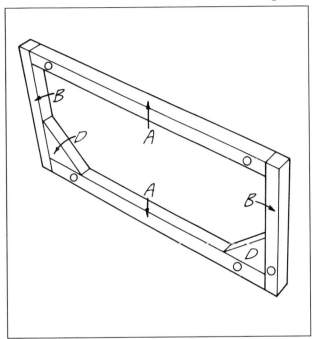

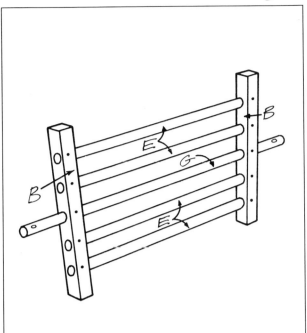

Figure I

ure **H**. (Do not use either of the **G** dowels that have four drilled holes.) Insert the dowel through the two center holes, leaving equal extensions on each side, and DO NOT glue the dowel in place or secure it with screws. It will be glued to the side sections later, but if you glue it to the **B** uprights of the back section you will not be able to pivot the section in the swing.

4. The assembled seat section is shown in **Figure I**. Assemble it as you did the back section, using the nine remaining **E** dowels in the nine center holes, one of the remaining **G** dowels at the back, and the **F** dowel at the front. Be sure that the side **C** members are turned the right way end for end, and that you have indeed inserted the **G** dowel through the holes closest to the ends marked as "back." Adjust the pieces so that the ends of the **E** dowels are flush with the outer edges of the **C** members, and the **F** and **G** dowels each extend equally on each side. Rotate the **G** dowel so that the holes run vertically, and secure each of the dowels using glue and screws as you did for the back section. The side from which you insert the screws will be the bottom. There's no need to leave any of the dowels unsecured, as the seat section should not pivot.

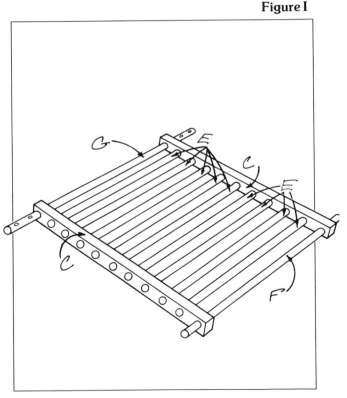

Final Assembly

The completely assembled swing is shown in **Figure J**. Refer to this diagram as you perform the assembly steps in this section.

1. Begin by connecting the back and seat sections to one side section. For the back section, insert one extending end of the center **G** dowel through the hole near the back of the upper **A** member of the side section. Be sure that the back section is turned so that the side from which you inserted the screws is toward the back of the swing.

2. Connect the seat section to the same side section as shown in **Figure J**, turning the seat section so that the side from which you inserted the screws is at the bottom. Insert one extending end of the **G** dowel through the hole near the back of the lower **A** member of the side section, and insert the extending end of the front **F** dowel into the hole near the bottom of the front **B** member of the side section. The seat section will slant slightly upward toward the front, which is as it should be to keep swingers more securely in the swing.

3. Connect the seat and back sections to the remaining side section in the same manner.

4. Adjust the sections so that the sides are very close to the back and seat sections. Leave enough space on each side so that the back section can pivot, but there should be enough friction to hold the back section in any chosen position. On the seat section, glue the extending ends of the **F** and **G** dowels in place in the holes of the side sections. The ends of the **F** dowel should be flush with the outer surfaces of the side sections, and should be trimmed if they extend beyond. Secure the **G** and **F** dowels by inserting screws through the frame members into the dowels. On the back section, rotate the **G** dowel so that the holes run vertically and are aligned with the inner holes in the seat-section **G** dowel directly below it. Be sure that the back-section **G** dowel extends equally beyond each side section, and glue it into the holes in the side sections. Do this carefully, because if the glue seeps out between the members of the side and back sections, you will not be able to pivot the back section. Actually, it is not necessary to glue this dowel. Secure each end by inserting a screw up through the **A** member of the side frame into the dowel.

5. Underneath the front of the seat section, insert the remaining **G** dowel through the hole near the front of the **A** member of one side section. Slide it through until you can guide it through the corresponding hole in the opposite side section. Adjust the dowel, leaving equal extensions on each side of the frame, rotate it so that the small holes run vertically, and glue it in place. Secure the dowel in place by inserting a screw up through the lower edge of the **A** piece into the dowel, on each side section of the frame.

6. Insert one of the **H** dowels into the hole near the front of the upper **A** member of one side section, as shown in **Figure J**. If you did not mark the outer and inner ends of the **H** dowels, be sure that the end closest to the hole is on the outside. The inner end should be flush with the inside of the **A** member. Rotate the dowel so the hole runs vertically, glue the dowel in place, and secure it by inserting a screw up through the **A** member into the dowel. Install the remaining **H** dowel on the opposite side of the swing.

7. Insert an **I** peg through the outermost hole in each of the lower **G** dowels, on each side of the swing. Glue the pegs in place, adjusting each one so that it extends equally on each side of the dowel.

8. Cut a 2-yard length of ski rope and thread it through the aligned holes in the upper and lower **G** dowels at the back of the swing on one side. Wrap one end around the lower dowel and tie or splice it securely. Pull up the slack so all the excess rope is above the upper dowel. (If you're not confident of your knot-tying, consult an expert. We called in the Boy Scouts.) Perform the same procedures at the front of the swing on the same side, using another 2-yard length of rope. Tie together the upper ends of the two ropes, and then repeat all of these procedures on the other side of the swing, using two additional 2-yard lengths of rope. Finally, cut two additional lengths of rope, each a yard or two longer than the distance from the top of the swing to the porch ceiling or tree branch from which you wish to hang it. On one side of the swing, tie one of these ropes to the two ropes already attached, where they are tied together. Use the second rope in the same manner on the opposite side of the swing. Tie these ropes to the tree branch or to the porch-ceiling hangers, which you probably haven't yet bought.

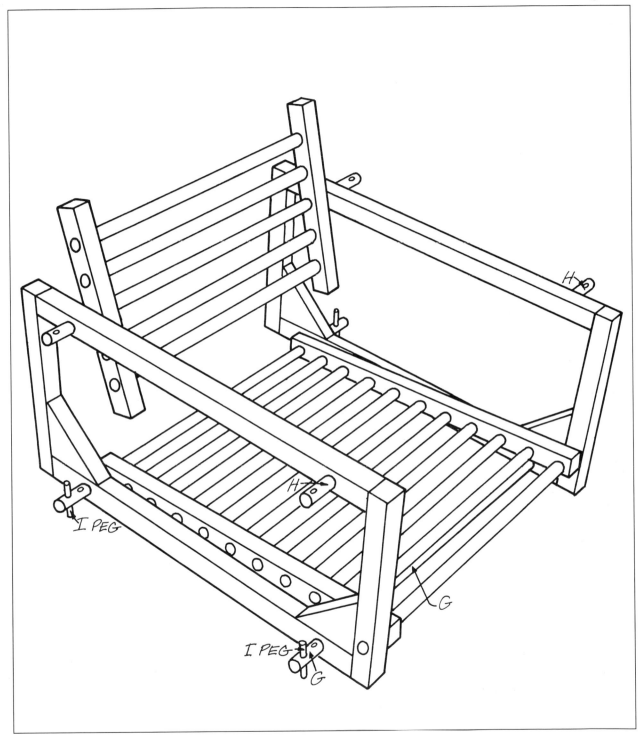

Picnic Table

This handsome, sturdy picnic table will last a lifetime and is constructed entirely of 2 x 4 redwood lumber. All you have to do is cut the required parts to length, make a few additional miter cuts, and you're ready for the easy-as-pie assembly. The tabletop measures 32 x 72 inches, and stands 32 inches above ground level. Each bench top measures 12 x 60, and stands 17 inches tall. Joints secured with removable bolts allow the structure to be disassembled for storage or transport.

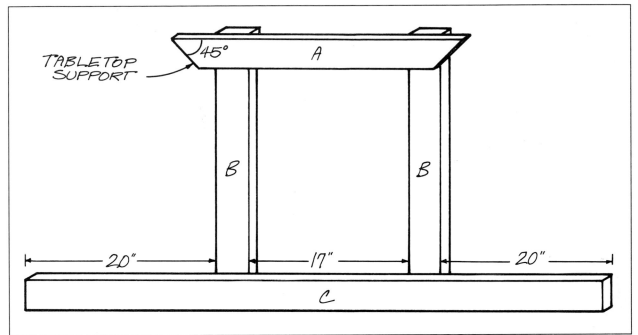

Materials

Fourteen 2 x 4 redwood boards, each 10 feet long

Forty-eight roundhead carriage bolts, each 3½ inches long and ¼ inch in diameter, with a flat washer and nut to fit

Seventy-six No. 12 gauge flathead wood screws, each 2½ inches long

A few 6d common nails to use in temporary assemblies

Constructing this picnic table is a real breeze. The support structure consists of two identical end sections connected by five braces. The tabletop and bench tops consist of 2 x 4 slats laid in parallel across the supports and secured with screws. All you have to do is cut the boards to length – no ripping required – and connect them as shown.

Cutting the Boards

1. All of the parts required to build the table are listed here. Cut the parts and label each with its identifying code referring to the cutting suggestions that follow.

Code	Length	Quantity
A	31 inches	2
B	30 inches	4
C	64 inches	2
D	12 inches	4
E	15½ inches	8
F	33 inches	3
G	34 inches	2
H	60 inches	6
I	72 inches	8

a. Cut each of three boards in half to form two 5-foot lengths. This will give you the six H pieces.

b. From each of four boards, cut one I piece, one B piece, and one E piece.

c. From each of two boards, cut one I piece and two E pieces.

d. From each of two boards, cut one I piece and one G piece.

e. From each of two boards, cut one C piece, one A piece, and two D pieces.

f. From the remaining board, cut the three F pieces.

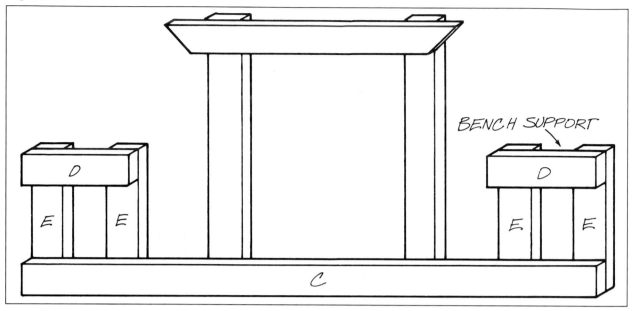

2. The A pieces will serve as the top supports of the two end sections. Miter both ends of each A piece at a 45-degree angle as shown in **Figure A**.

Building the End Sections

1. Begin assembling one end section by building a structure like the one shown in **Figure A**, using temporary holding nails to join the pieces. Allow a 17-inch space between the two B pieces, and position the A and C pieces so they both extend equally beyond each B piece. The A and B pieces should be flush at the top, and the B and C pieces should be flush at the bottom.

2. To accommodate the bolts, drill two 5/16-inch-diameter holes through the boards at each intersection. After you have drilled the first hole, remove the temporary holding nail and use the opening as the position for the second bolt, so you do not end up with an extra hole in the wood at each intersection. Insert the bolts and secure each one with a washer and nut.

3. Now add a bench support to each end of the C piece as shown in **Figure B**, using temporary nails as you did for the center portion. Each bench support consists of one D and two E pieces. The outer E piece of each support should be flush with the end of the C piece, and each D piece should fit evenly across the two

E pieces. Drill the bolt holes and install the bolts as you did in step 2.

4. Repeat the procedures in steps 1 through 3 to build a second, identical end section.

Joining the End Sections

The two end sections are joined using three connecting braces and two angled supports (**Figure C**).

1. To begin, align the two end sections approximately 3 feet apart, and insert an F piece between the two bench supports at each side. Each end of the F piece should be halfway between the two legs of the bench support at that end. Secure each joint by inserting two screws through the C piece, into the end of the F piece.

2. Insert the remaining F piece between the two A pieces at the top and secure each end using two screws.

3. The two G pieces serve as the angled supports and must be mitered at the ends as shown in **Figure D**. Miter each G piece, being careful to cut the angles on the correct sides at the end with a double miter.

4. Install the G pieces as shown in **Figure C**. Secure the joints using two screws inserted through each G piece into the F piece at the top, and two screws in-

Figure C

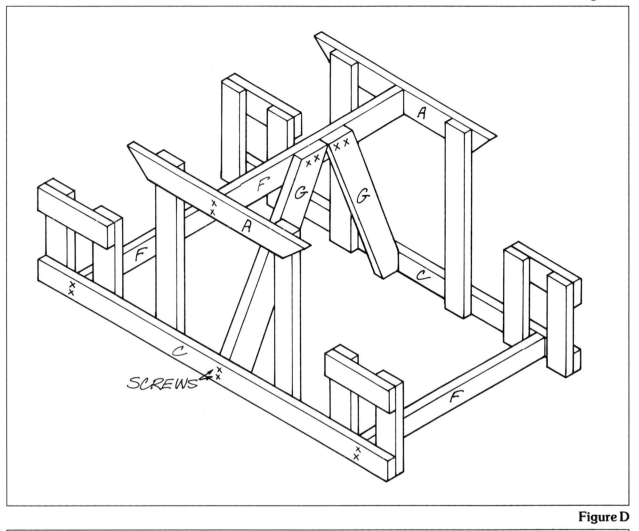

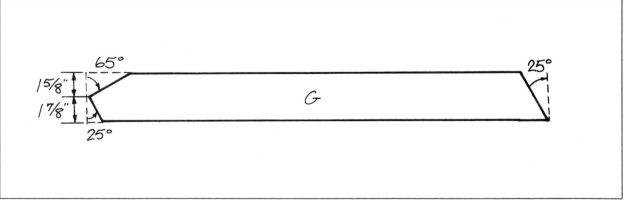

PICNIC TABLE

Figure E

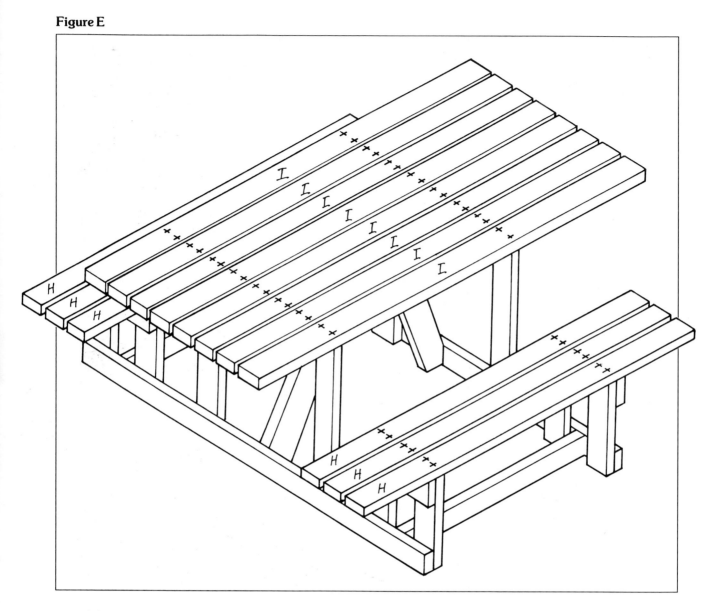

serted through each C piece into the mitered edge of the G piece at the bottom.

Final Assembly

1. To form the tabletop, place the eight I pieces across the supports as shown in **Figure E**, allowing a ½-inch space between slats. They should extend equally beyond the supports at each end. Secure each slat using two screws inserted down through the slat and into the support near each end.

2. To form one bench top, place three H pieces across the two bench supports on one side of the table as shown in **Figure E**, allowing a ¾-inch space between slats. Adjust them so that they extend equally beyond each bench support and secure with screws as you did the tabletop slats. Install the remaining three H pieces across the bench supports on the opposite side of the table.

The Round Table

The only knights associated with this round table will be enjoyable summer ones. It includes a wooden lazy Susan to help you pass the iced tea around the 60-inch-diameter tabletop, and four curved benches.

Materials

For the table:

70 linear feet of redwood 2 x 6

14 linear feet of redwood 2 x 2

14 linear feet of redwood 2 x 4

12 linear feet of redwood 1 x 8

Flathead wood screws: No. 12 gauge, 2½ inches long; No. 6 gauge, 1½ inches long; and No. 18 gauge, 3½ inches long

Umbrella: The table was designed to be used with a standard patio-table umbrella – the type that has a conical metal base, which can be filled with sand for ballast. The base can be as tall as 8 inches and as wide as 16 inches in diameter across the bottom.

For the lazy Susan:

10 linear feet of redwood 1 x 8

3 linear feet of redwood or other 1 x 10 stock for the trim (We used pine for contrast.)

13 x 13-inch piece of ¼-inch exterior plywood

Five small ball-bearing casters, ½ to ⅝ inch high and ½ to ¾ inch in diameter

3d finishing nails

A lazy Susan base, which is a round, two-layered metal contraption that contains a ball-bearing mechanism. The upper layer can be rotated while the lower layer remains stationary. The one we purchased was 12 inches in diameter. You'll also need a few ½-inch-long flathead wood screws.

For the benches:

The quantities specified below are sufficient to build four benches, which will fit nicely around the table.

63 linear feet of redwood 2 x 6

7 linear feet of redwood 2 x 2

No. 6 gauge, 1½-inch-long flathead wood screws

3d finishing nails

4d common nails

THE TABLE

The round table may look sort of complex, but it really is not. The tabletop consists of 2 x 6 slats secured underneath by cross braces. Each leg is basically an L-shaped assembly of 2 x 6 boards, attached to a thinner support. When joined together, the four thinner supports (one for each leg assembly) form a square center post that accommodates the umbrella shaft.

Figure A

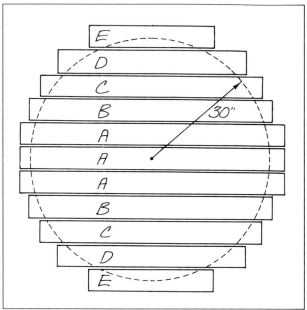

Cutting the parts

1. Cut the parts listed below from redwood 2 x 6 and label each with its identifying code.

Code	Length	Quantity
A	60 inches	3
B	57½ inches	2
C	53 inches	2
D	45 inches	2
E	31 inches	2
F	24½ inches	4
G	21 inches	4
H	5½ inches	4

2. The A through E pieces will serve as the tabletop slats and must be trimmed to form a circle. Place them side by side as shown in **Figure A**, allowing a small space (about ⅛ inch or so) between slats. Examine each slat and turn it best side down. Draw the outline of a 60-inch-diameter circle on the boards, using the center point of the middle A piece as the center of the circle. (A really easy way to do this is to temporarily nail one end of a yardstick to the center point, measure along the yardstick 30 inches from the nail, and drill a

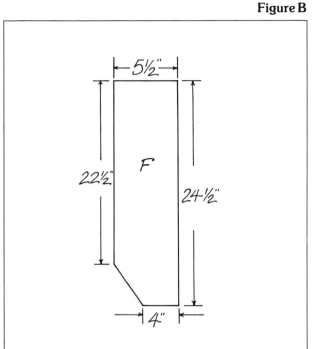

Figure C

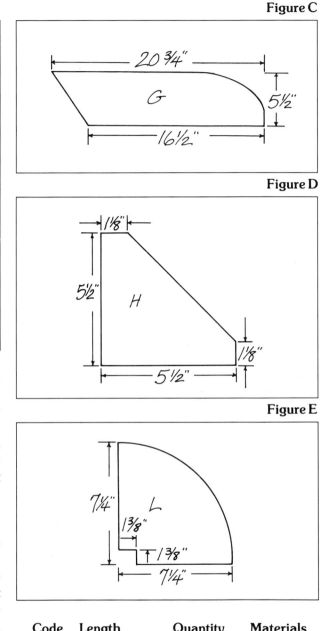

small hole through the yardstick at that point. Insert the point of a pencil through the drilled hole, and rotate the yardstick around the boards to draw the circle.) Now trim the ends of the boards along the outline. Finally, drill a hole through the exact center of the middle **A** piece to accommodate the umbrella shaft. The hole should be just slightly larger in diameter than the shaft of the umbrella.

3. The F pieces will serve as the legs and must be mitered at one end to accommodate the umbrella base. A cutting diagram is provided in **Figure B**. Cut off one corner of each F piece as shown.

4. The G pieces will serve as the feet. They must be mitered to accommodate the legs and rounded off at the outer ends for a more attractive look. A cutting diagram for the foot is provided in **Figure C**. Modify each G piece as shown.

5. The H pieces will serve as corner blocks in the leg assemblies and must be mitered. A cutting diagram is provided in **Figure D**. Cut one corner of each H piece as shown.

6. Cut the remaining parts for the table as listed at right, using the specified materials. Label each part.

Code	Length	Quantity	Materials
I	56 inches	2	2 x 2
J	10 inches	4	2 x 2
K	58 inches	2	2 x 4
L	7¼ inches	4	1 x 8
M	22¼ inches	4	1 x 8
N	15¼ inches	2	2 x 4

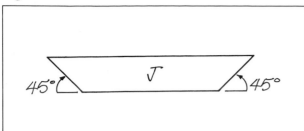

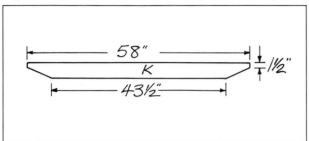

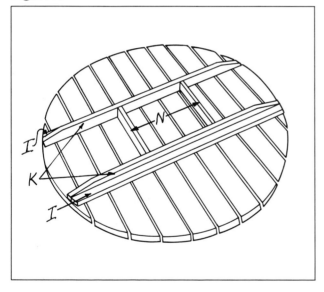

7. From the remaining 1 x 8 cut three square pieces, each 2¾ x 2¾ inches. These will serve as spacers inside the center post that is formed when the four leg assemblies are joined. Drill a hole through the exact center of each spacer to accommodate the umbrella shaft. Label each center post spacer O.

8. The L pieces will serve as decorative (and functional) leg spacers and must be notched to fit the legs. A cutting diagram is provided in **Figure E**. The curved outer edge is one-quarter of a 14½-inch-diameter circle, which you can draw on the L pieces using the same yardstick technique that we used for the tabletop. In addition, cut the corner notch as shown. Modify each of the L pieces in this manner.

9. The J pieces will serve as supports for the leg spacers. Miter both ends of each J piece at a 45-degree angle as shown in **Figure F**.

10. The M pieces are ripped to create the center post sides. Make one rip cut straight through each M piece, 2¾ inches from one long edge. Measure the widths of the two resulting boards, and trim if necessary to get two 22¼-inch-long boards: one 2¾ inches wide and one 4¼ inches wide. Label both the boards M. Rip all four M pieces in this manner, and label each of the boards M.

11. The K pieces will serve as tabletop braces and should be mitered as shown in **Figure G**. Miter both K pieces in this manner.

Constructing the Tabletop

1. Align the tabletop slats A through E as you did when you trimmed them, best sides down. Place the two K braces crosswise on top, 15¼ inches apart, equally distant from the center of the tabletop. Each K brace should be resting on its longest edge, and the ends should be flush with the edge of the tabletop. Slide the two N braces between the K braces as shown, spacing them as you did the K braces, 15¼ inches apart and equally distant from the center of the tabletop. Glue the joints and insert screws through the K braces into the ends of the N braces.

2. Place an I piece along the outer side of each K brace as shown in **Figure H**. These pieces should be a little longer than the tabletop, so adjust them to leave equal extensions beyond each edge. Glue them in place and secure with screws inserted up into the tabletop slats (use two screws for each slat on each I brace, except for the short outer slats which can do with one apiece per brace). Insert additional screws through the K braces into the I pieces. Trim the ends of the I braces flush with the edge of the tabletop.

Figure I

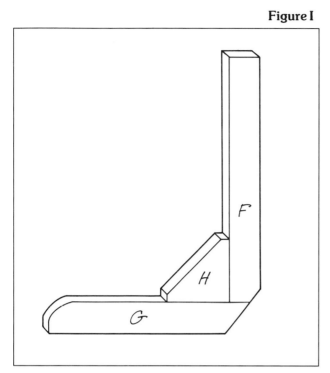

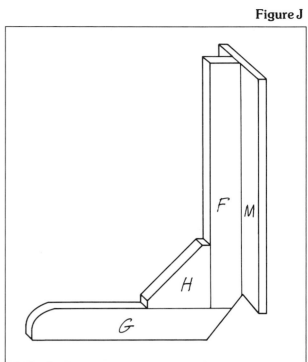

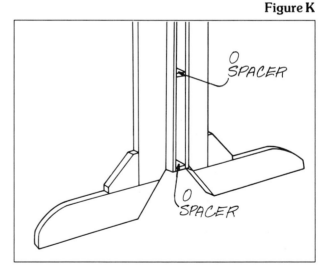

Constructing the Legs

1. The basic leg assembly is shown in **Figure I**. The joints should be splined. Assemble one F, one G, and one H piece as shown and secure by angling screws through the foot G up into the leg F, and through the corner block H into both the leg and foot.

2. Construct three identical leg assemblies, using the remaining F, G, and H pieces.

3. Glue one of the center post sides M to one of the leg assemblies, along the short edge of the leg as shown in **Figure J**. It doesn't matter whether you use a wide or narrow post side. The upper ends of the F and M pieces should be even and the lower end of the M piece should be flush with the mitered corner as shown. The leg should be centered between the long edges of the M piece. Secure the joint by inserting screws through the post side M into the edge of the leg.

4. Attach an M piece to each remaining leg assembly in the same manner. Each leg should be centered along one of the M pieces, whether it's a wide or narrow post side M.

Assembling the Base

1. Find the two leg assemblies that include the narrower M post sides and place them back to back (M piece to M piece). Slide them apart until you can insert one of the O center post spacers between them as

Figure L

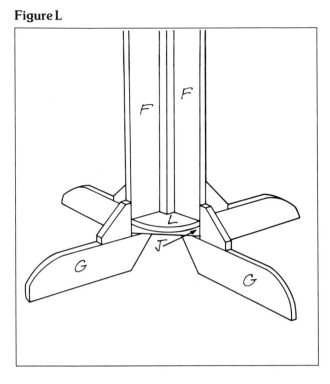

shown in **Figure K**. Place the spacer about midway between the top and bottom ends of the post sides. Glue it in place and secure with screws through the **M** pieces.

2. Insert a second **O** spacer between the legs flush with the lower ends of the post pieces, and a third flush with the upper ends. Glue and secure these **O** spacers in the same manner.

3. Place one of the remaining legs against one side of this assembly. The wider post side **M** should fit perfectly up against the edges of the two narrower post sides that are already joined by the spacers. Glue the joints and insert screws through the wider **M** piece into the edges of the other post sides.

4. Attach the fourth leg assembly to the center post sides in the same manner.

5. Now add the leg spacers **L** and supports **J** as shown in **Figure L**. Glue a **J** support between the **F** members of two of the leg assemblies, placing it just above the **F**-to-**G** joints. Secure the ends with screws. Place an **L** spacer on top as shown, glue it in place, and secure with screws.

6. Attach one **J** support and one **L** spacer between

each two legs in the same manner. When you get to the space between the final pair of legs, you'll have to insert the screws at an angle.

Final Assembly

The assembled table will be fairly heavy, and certainly unwieldy, so we suggest that you perform the final assembly where you want the table to stay. First, place the assembled base over the metal umbrella stand. Place the tabletop over the assembled base as shown in the bottom-view drawing, **Figure M**. The top of the base structure should just fit inside the square formed by the tabletop braces **K** and **N**. Secure the joints by inserting screws down through the tabletop slats into the upper ends of the legs **F**. Insert the umbrella shaft down through the hole in the tabletop, which, if everything got cut and assembled correctly, will be perfectly aligned with the holes in the center post spacers. The umbrella shaft undoubtedly will slide smoothly down through the post and into its base, where it will live happily ever after – or at least until you have to remove it in order to insert...

THE LAZY SUSAN

This is a very simple structure, consisting of a round platter with edge trim. It is mounted on the lazy Susan base hardware.

Cutting the Parts

1. Cut the parts listed below from redwood 1 x 8 and label each with its code.

Code	Length	Quantity
P	28 inches	2
Q	25 inches	2

2. the **P** and **Q** pieces will be joined together and trimmed to form the platter. It's best if you spline the joints along the edges for a smoother appearance and a longer-lasting structure. Edge-join the **P** and **Q** pieces in the order shown in **Figure N**, using glued spline joints (see Tips & Techniques). Clamp overnight.

3. Draw the outline of a 28-inch-diameter circle on the splined platter boards as shown in **Figure N**, using

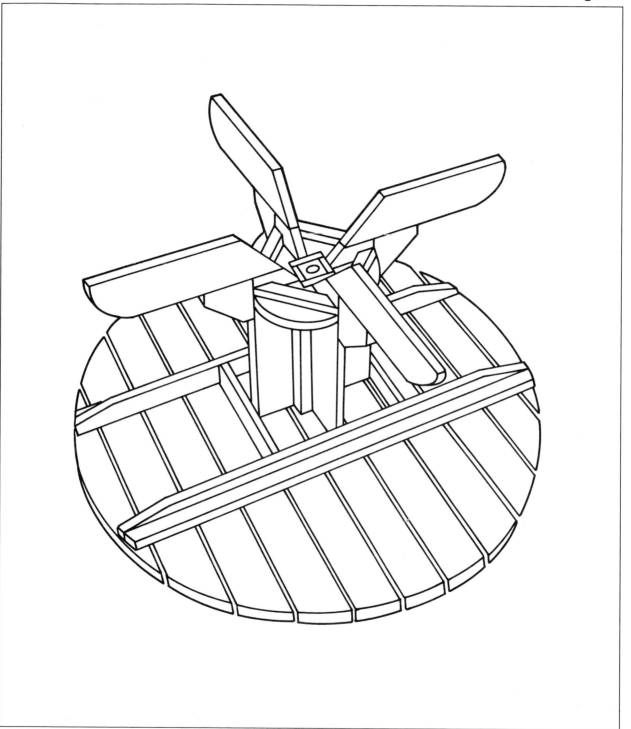

THE ROUND TABLE

Figure N

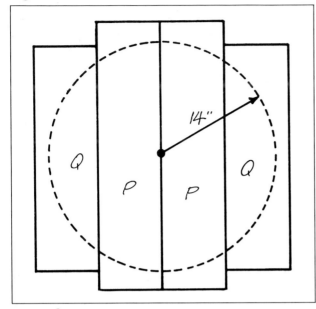

Figure O

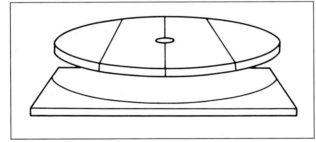

Figure P

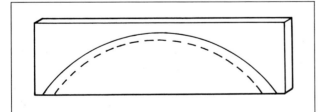

Figure Q

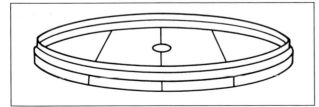

the midpoint between the two P pieces as the center of the circle. Trim the ends of the boards along the outline.

4. Drill a hole straight down through the center of the platter, to accommodate the umbrella shaft.

5. The plywood is used as a base for the lazy Susan hardware. Place the hardware right side up on the plywood and trace around the lower plate. Cut the plywood along the outline. Drill a hole through the center of the plywood, to accommodate the umbrella shaft.

6. You'll notice that the bottom plate of the lazy Susan hardware contains several holes. These are access holes that allow you to insert a screw driver through the bottom plate in order to reach the screws that attach the upper plate to the platter. Drill a hole through the plywood base, matching the placement of one of the access holes in the lazy Susan lower plate. Glue the plywood base to the lower plate, matching access holes.

7. The platter trim is cut in separate sections from the 1 x 10 stock. To cut the first section, place the redwood platter on top of the 1 x 10, placing the edge of the platter as close as possible to one long edge of the stock (**Figure O**). Trace along the curved edge of the platter. Remove the platter and cut the 1 x 10 along the traced outline. Cut the 1 x 10 again, ¾ inch inside the first curved line as shown in **Figure P**. The resulting curved piece, ¾ inch wide, is the first trim section.

8. The second trim section is cut from the semi-circular piece of the 1 x 10 that is left over from step 7. Place the platter on top and trace the curve as you did before. (Note that you can not use the existing curved edge of the leftover stock as the first cut for this trim section, as it is a smaller curve than the edge of the platter.) Cut along the traced outline, and again ¾ inch inside the first cut line as you did before. This is the second trim section, which will be shorter than the first one.

9. Repeat the procedures in step 8 to cut a third trim section. The three sections should be sufficient to reach all the way around the platter. If not, cut a fourth trim section in the same manner.

10. We ran each trim section through the shaper to create a bead design along the outside curve as shown in the assembly diagram, **Figure Q**.

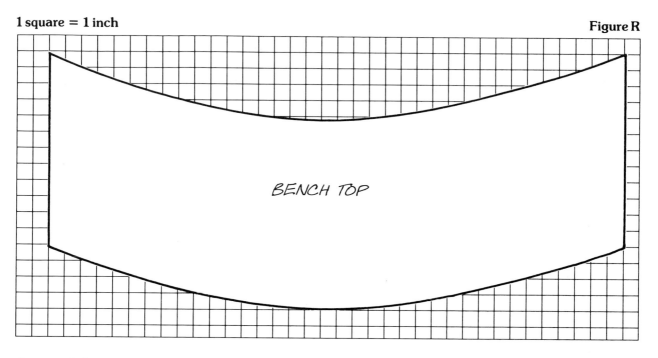

BENCH TOP

Assembly

1. Begin by attaching the lazy Susan hardware to the underside of the platter. Place the hardware in the exact center, rotating the bottom layer until the access hole is aligned with one of the screw holes in the top layer. Insert a screw through the hole, into the platter. Rotate the lower layer to align the access hole with a second screw hole, etc. Use at least three screws to secure the assembly in this manner.

2. The ball-bearing casters will keep the platter from rocking. Attach them to the underside of the platter, evenly spaced about 1 inch from the edge.

3. The trim sections are attached to the top of the platter, flush with the edge as shown in **Figure Q**. Arrange the trim pieces as shown and miter the ends to fit together. Glue the trim in place and drive finishing nails up through the platter into the trim pieces.

4. Place the lazy Susan on the round table and insert the umbrella shaft through the center holes.

THE BENCHES

The bench assembly is quite simple. Each leg is composed of two 2 x 6 boards splined together. The bench top consists of three 2 x 6 boards cut to form the curve.

Cutting the Parts

1. Cut the parts listed below from the specified materials and label each part with its code. The quantities listed are sufficient for four benches.

Code	Length	Quantity	Material
R	36 inches	12	2 x 6
S	16 inches	16	2 x 6
T	9 inches	8	2 x 2

2. The R pieces will serve as the seat slats and must be contoured to form the curved bench tops. Place three R pieces side by side, with the long edges glued together. Enlarge the scale drawing for the bench top provided in **Figure R**, and use the full-size pattern to contour the bench top to the proper shape. Repeat these procedures to glue together and contour three more bench tops, using the remaining R pieces.

3. Each bench top must be dadoed on the underside to accommodate the legs. A cutting diagram is provided in **Figure S**. Refer to the diagram as you cut or rout two dadoes across the underside of one bench top, making each dado ¾ inch deep and 1½ inches wide. Modify the three remaining bench tops in the same manner.

Figure S

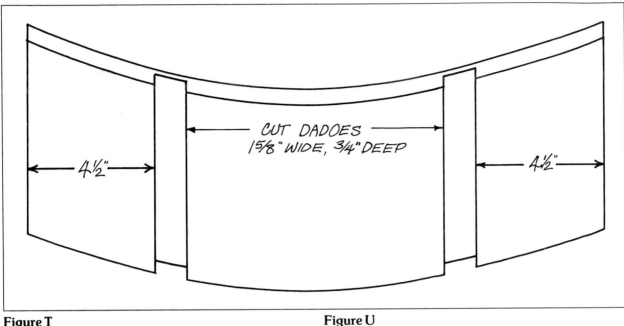

CUT DADOES
1⁵⁄₈" WIDE, ³⁄₄" DEEP

4½"

4½"

Figure T

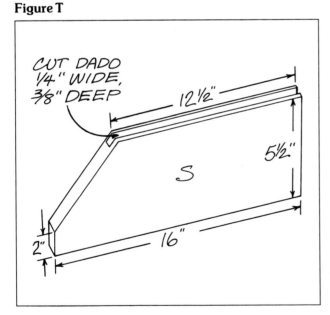

CUT DADO
¼" WIDE,
³⁄₈" DEEP

12½"

5½"

S

16"

2"

Figure U

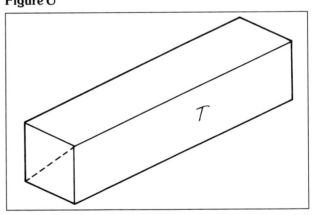

T

along the shortened edge as shown, to accommodate the spline. The dado should be ¼ inch wide and ³⁄₈ inch deep, cut along the center of the edge. Modify each of the S pieces in the same manner.

5. The splines are cut from scrap redwood, but the stock must first be planed or ripped to a thickness of ¼ inch. Cut eight splines from the planed stock, each 1¼ inches wide and 12½ inches long.

6. The T pieces will serve as glue blocks to strengthen the seat-to-leg joints. Cut each T piece in half along the diagonal as shown in **Figure U**. Label each half T.

4. The S pieces will serve as the legs. Each bench has two legs, and each leg consists of two S pieces splined together as shown in the assembly diagram, **Figure V**. Begin by mitering one corner of each S piece as shown in the cutting diagram, **Figure T**. In addition, cut a dado

BUILDING OUTDOOR FURNITURE

Assembly

1. To assemble one leg, join two **S** pieces using one of the splines as shown in **Figure V**. There should be about ½ inch of the spline showing between the **S** pieces. Glue the spline in place and secure by inserting a few finishing nails through each **S** piece into the spline. Assemble seven more legs in the same manner, using the remaining **S** pieces and splines.

2. Temporarily assemble one bench as shown in **Figure W**, placing the bench top over two legs and inserting the upper ends of the legs into the dadoes in the underside of the bench top. Don't add the glue blocks just yet. Note that the legs are slightly wider than the bench top. Mark the outlines of the curved bench top edges on the upper end of each leg. Disassemble the bench and bevel the long outer edges of the legs, following the marks you made on the upper ends.

3. Reassemble the bench, glueing the legs into the bench-top dadoes, and add the glue blocks as shown in **Figure W**, one on each side of each leg. Insert screws down through the bench top into the ends of the legs, and toenail up through the glue blocks into the bench top using common nails.

4. Repeat the procedures in steps 2 and 3 to assemble three more benches, and get ready for some legendary nights around the round table.

Figure V

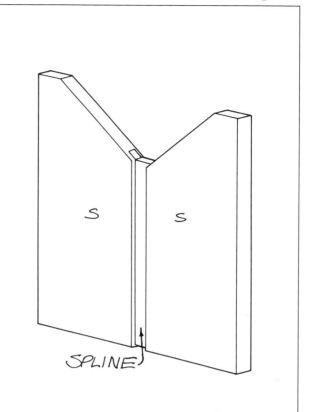

Figure W

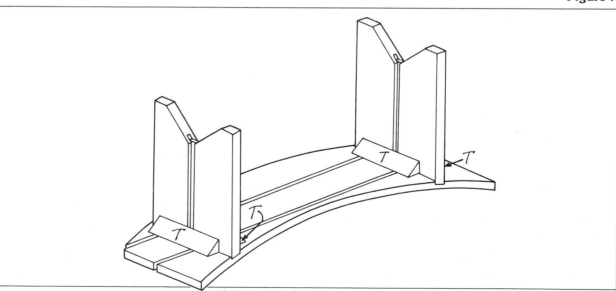